The BigBridge Book of Contemporary Indian Poetry
(2013, 2015)

The BigBridge Book of Contemporary Indian Poetry
(2013, 2015)

Edited by
Menka Shivdasani

Foreword by
Michael Rothenberg

BLACK EAGLE BOOKS
Dublin, USA | Bhubaneswar, India

Black Eagle Books
USA Address:
7464 Wisdom Lane
Dublin, OH 43016

India Address:
E/312, Trident Galaxy, Kalinga Nagar,
Bhubaneswar-751003, Odisha, India

E-mail: info@blackeaglebooks.org
Website: www.blackeaglebooks.org

First International Edition Published by
Black Eagle Books, 2024

THE BIGBRIDGE BOOK OF CONTEMPORARY INDIAN POETRY
Edited by **Menka Shivdasani**
https://menkashivdasani.in

Foreword by **Michael Rothenberg**

Copyright © **Menka Shivdasani**

All rights reserved. No part of this publication may be reproduced, stored in a retrieval system, or transmitted, in any form or by any means, electronic, mechanical, photocopying, recording or otherwise without the prior permission of the publisher.

Interior Design: **Ezy's Publication**
Cover Photography & Design: Copyright 2024 © **Sudeep Sen**

ISBN- 978-1-64560-558-4 (Paperback)
Library of Congress Control Number: 2024942982

Printed in the United States of America

For Michael Rothenberg (1951 – 2022)

Other books by Menka Shivdasani

Poetry
Nirvana at Ten Rupees, XAL-Praxis, 1990
Stet, Sampark, 2000
Safe House, Paperwall Media and Publishing, 2015
Frazil (1980 – 2017), Paperwall Media and Publishing

Translations / Bilingual books
Freedom and Fissures, Sahitya Akademi, 1990
Brittle Ice, Copper Coin, 2015
While Sowing Dreams, Black and White Fountain, 2023
The Seven Queens: Sindhi Folktales in English Verse by Menka Shivdasani, translated into Sindhi by Barkha Khushalani, Black Eagle Books, 2024

Books Edited
BigBridge Anthology of Contemporary Indian Poetry: Part 1 2013; Part 2 2015 (online)
If the Roof Leaks, Let it Leak, SPARROW, 2014

Corporate History/ Non-Fiction
18 books, co-authored/ edited with with Raju Kane, including:

Reach for the Stars: The Story of Blue Star Limited, 2018
A Legacy of Learning: Hyderabad (Sind) National Collegiate Board - 7 Decades, 2022

CONTENTS

Anthology of Contemporary Indian Poetry I (2013)

ADIL JUSSAWALLA
Poker-Faced 25
A Bomb-site Seen from a Railway Bridge 27
Her Safe House 28

ARVIND KRISHNA MEHROTRA
Approaching Fifty 29
The Sale 30

EUNICE de SOUZA
Conversation Piece 33
Advice to Women 34
From My Mother Feared Death 35

GIEVE PATEL
How Do You Withstand, Body 36
Post-Mortem 37
Squirrels in Washington 38

KEKI N. DARUWALLA
At War 39
Filming 40
Defining a Sufi 41

K. SATCHIDANANDAN
Burnt Poems 43
Old Women 45
The Fox 47

MALAY ROYCHOUDHURY
Chicken Roast 49
Preparation 50
Throne of the Weevil 52

ANAMIKA
Without a Place 53
Mobile 55

RANDHIR KHARE
I Do Not Know You, City 57
Unknown Soldier 59
Camilla 60

JEET THAYIL
Poem with Prediction 61
From Premonition (*for Shakti*) 63

MANOHAR SHETTY
Elegy 66
Animal Planet 67
Closure 69

HEMANT DIVATE
A Depressingly Monotonous Landscape (*for Hiranya*) 71
Something about This Shore for the
Poet of the Shore Beyond (*for Dilip Chitre*) 75

TABISH KHAIR
Rumi and the Reed 78
South Delhi Murder 79
Almost a Ghazal: For My Grandfather's Garden 81

HOSHANG MERCHANT
My Sister Takes a Long Long Time to Die 82
Ashes of Gandhi 84
Scent of Love 88

ANJU MAKHIJA
Pickling Season 90
A Farmer's Ghost 91

SAMPURNA CHATTARJI
Where Do I Put This Love 92
(*for Calcutta*), the city I left behind
No Shape Is More Constant 94
for Revathy Gopal (1947-2007)

TISHANI DOSHI
Cutting Broccoli 97
That Woman 98
Love Poem 99

SUDEEP SEN
Bharatanatyam Dancer 100
Kargil 102

GAYATRI MAJUMDAR
Light Shift 104
Tribute to Revolutionaries 106

ANNIE ZAIDI
Cine Sestina 108
City, Twilight 110
Lifer Giving Advice to New Convict in Female Ward 112

ARUNDHATHI SUBRAMANIAM
5.46, Andheri Local 114
The City and I 115

SHIKHANDIN
Cliffs of Moher on Alien Lips 117
We Met for Beer and Metastasis 119
Black Tar Road 121

PRIYA SARUKKAI CHABRIA
The Gathering of Time – Dialogues with Kalidasa 123
Poems from Babylon and Persia 124
Refuse/ Refused: Fragments from Three Cantos 126

JERRY PINTO
I Want a Poem 127
Alt-Ctrl-Dlt 129
House Repairs 130

MEENA KANDASAMY
Passion Becomes Piety 131
Six Hours of Chastity 132

LAKSMISREE BANERJEE
Haria 134
Peahen Passions 136
Gandhi at the Crossroads 137

ANAND THAKORE
The Koh-i-noor 138
Nineteen Forty-Two 141

HARISH NAMBIAR
Uncalled for 143
Widows of Benares 144

ABHA IYENGAR
The Way Out 146
Torn and Stitched 147

VIHANG A. NAIK
The Banyan City 149

SMITA AGARWAL
Transformations 151
Angrezi Vangrezi 153

K SRILATA
Not in the Picture 155
The Big Elephant in My Room 158

ANUPAMA RAJU
Ganesha's Ghazal 159
The Time-Eater 160

MUSTANSIR DALVI
Why Someone Needed to Kick
the Infant Kafka in the Balls 161
Prayer Can Change Your Fate, Too 162

RIZIO YOHANNAN RAJ
Digambara 164
Daughter 165

TANYA MENDONSA
Daughters of the Lie 167
I Sing a Song of Goa 169

MENKA SHIVDASANI
Why Rabbits Never Sleep 172
Tea Party 174

Anthology of Contemporary Indian Poetry II (2015)

ABHAY K
Chitwan 177
Nagarkot 178
Bandipur 179

ANITA NAIR
In Which a Small Gesture Becomes Epic 180
How Men Eat 184

ANJALI PUROHIT
The Wave 187
The Wave Answers 189
Shades of Grey 191

ANNA SUJATHA MATHAI
Light 193
A Small Death – A Small Joy 194

BARNALI RAY SHUKLA
Palash and the Padmini 195

DEEPANKAR KHIWANI
Who Knows 197
The Vampire of the Underground 199

DION D'SOUZA
Angulimala 200
For T., who Likens Me to a Rock 201
King 203

DOMINIC ALAPAT
When We Meet 204
In Search 205

GJV PRASAD
Growing Old 207
Road Kill 208

GOPIKRISHNAN KOTTOOR
The Mad Woman in the Shiva Temple 209
The Passport 211

JENNIFER ROBERTSON
To Kiss Like Caravaggio 213
Dimensions of a Swimming Pool for Narcissus 214

LINDA ASHOK
On His Second Marriage 216
Hard Water 217

MALSAWMI JACOB
Zorami 218

MANI RAO
Postcard Aphrodite 219
Fêted 223

MANISHA LAKHE
Good Intentions 227

NABINA DAS
Poems from Rivers and Towns:
Fireflies and Fish Conversations 229

ROCHELLE POTKAR
Transmogrified 232
Raw Forms 233

SARABJEET GARCHA
The Gurdwara with a Bell 235
Mountain Maker 237

SHIKHA MALAVIYA
Hiraeth 239
Genocide Gatehouse 241

SRIDALA SWAMI
Daybreak 243
Red Chillies 244
No Thirteen Ways About It 245

UMA NARAYAN
Terminus 246

USHA AKELLA
Bridges of Struga 248
Jerusalem 250
The Rosary of Latitudes 252

THE CONTRIBUTORS 255

Contemporary Indian Poetry: Like an *Abhang*, Unfinished

MENKA SHIVDASANI

In 2013, the United States-based poet Michael Rothenberg asked if I would be willing to put together an anthology of Indian poetry for the prestigious twenty-year-old literary e-zine he edited, *www.bigbridge.org*. I knew this would be a mammoth task because the landscape was vast; the number of poets writing in English had risen exponentially, and yet, they formed only a tiny microcosm of Indian poetry in general, which spans 22 official languages and an intricate literary tradition enriched over several centuries—Sanskrit literature that has its roots in the Rig Veda (1500-1200 BCE); classical Tamil Sangam literature (300 BCE to 300 CE); the *bhajans* of the Bhakti movement as exemplified by Meerabai (c. 1502 – c. 1552 AD) and the devotional *abhangs* in Marathi of Sant Tukaram in the 17th century, to name a few.

However, the thought of taking the richness of Indian writing to an international audience through a serious literary journal on the Internet excited me. While acutely aware of the limitations, I decided that while I would include a few of my favourite regional language poems in English translation, I would essentially focus on contemporary Indian poetry in English—a genre that Nissim Ezekiel, who passed away in 2004, had revitalised in the 1950s. I defined the word loosely to encompass writers who had brought fresh vigour and vitality to Indian poetry in English, introducing a new idiom in the 1960s and 1970s, and who were still writing actively in 2013; a few poems that contributed to this evolution first appeared in the 1970s and '80s. I included them to provide some sense of perspective and continuity. It would have been impossible, however, to include all the poets I would have liked in this anthology. Certainly, Jayanta Mahapatra, who passed away in August 2023, was among them; he was the first Indian poet to win a Sahitya Akademi Award for English poetry. Though I had known him in my early days, we had lost touch, and I was unable to connect with him at the time. There were also some other poets who did not respond to my request for their work.

I chose to keep the collection broad-based instead of narrowing it down to any particular theme. The global reach of an e-zine would mean that this anthology would connect with many who might be unfamiliar with Indian writing, and this would serve as some kind of introduction.

In 2015, when Michael asked if I would put together a second anthology, I readily agreed because many younger poets had remained unrepresented. This vibrant community – or should one say, these vibrant communities – now included several younger poets who were writing some powerful poetry.

In 2024, as I take another look at these two online anthologies for this print edition more than a decade after the first one appeared, I am aware that the landscape has expanded even further – that while the 'older' poets now in their 50s and 60s think it is time to bring out their collected works, there are many more youngsters who are filling the frame. The expanding café culture has provided spaces for Open Mics and spoken word poetry. As with all poetry, some of it is excellent, while other verses piggyback on the style of delivery and uninhibited themes to convince you of their literary worth. There are also several committed poet-publishers who have taken the genre to the wider universe, offering platforms that did not exist in the 1970s, when I first met the contemporary Indian English poets who were opening new doors to fledgling poets such as myself.

While few women writers made their presence felt in the 1970s, they have now made a significant difference to the tone and quality of Indian writing across languages. As Dr K V Raghupathi, convener of the National Seminar on Women Poets in Indian English Poetry, observed in March 2013 at the Central University of Tamil Nadu, poetry by women writers in post-colonial times has "organically responded to the Indian situation by raising questions related to self, identity, patriarchy, political and social consciousness. But visibility nonetheless remains a cause of concern, not only for the regional women poets but also for their Indian English counterparts". Organisations such as CS Lakshmi's Sound and Picture Archives for Research on Women (SPARROW) and, more recently, Smeetha Bhoumik's Woman Empowered (WE) have done much to foster this community of women writers.

Indian poets writing in English have earned their space on the global stage, forging new paths and moulding the language to suit the Indian landscape, concerns, and themes. When Nissim Ezekiel crossed new frontiers with his *'A Time to Change'* in 1952, it was recognised as one of the first significant books of postcolonial poetry in English;

decades later, however, sceptics continued to ask why Indians insisted on writing in English and not in their mother tongues. An exasperated Saleem Peeradina said to me in an interview soon after his debut poetry collection *First Offence* appeared in 1980, "This question should be outlawed!" Mercifully, though such discussions may still linger in some academic circles, the issue no longer merits attention, at least among poets.

Michael Rothenberg's request that I edit two anthologies—one in 2013 and the second in 2015—gave me the opportunity to engage with many poets who have been actively writing since the 1970s. This number has multiplied exponentially, and certainly, there is room for a third—or even a fourth—BigBridge anthology of contemporary Indian poets. It breaks my heart to think that this will not happen; Michael passed away on November 21, 2022. He had been waiting to see a print edition of these anthologies and had graciously written a Foreword for it, which he sent me on February 11, 2018. Towards the end of his life, Michael himself had several manuscripts awaiting publication—some of which saw the light of day to much acclaim.

Michael was an influential figure, the co-founder, with Terri Carrion, of the global movement 100 Thousand Poets for Change, which brought together a community of poets worldwide right from its first year in 2011. It is a precious legacy and continues to sustain many of us who have been associated with it. As Michael once said, speaking of 100 Thousand Poets for Change: "We are in a world where it isn't just one issue that needs to be addressed. A common ground is built through this global compilation of local stories, which is how we create a true narrative for discourse to inform the future."

A few months before he passed away, Michael sent me a long poem that he had written during his illness. In it, he spoke of gardenias and how they impacted his life.

I'd like to end this note with my tribute to him, a poem that I wrote when we lost him. Poets and poetry never die – their fragrance will last a lifetime, and their music, to borrow the poet Anamika's image, is like an *abhang* – creating a sense of kinship and free-flowing energy, but always unfinished, as it waits for the next magical notes that will keep the enchantment alive.

This anthology is for Michael and for the legacy he has left behind. It is also for the many poets included here who are no longer with us and to whom I owe so much during my own journey as a poet – among them, Gieve Patel, Eunice de Souza, Malay Roychoudhury, Vihang A. Naik, Anna Sujatha Mathai and Deepankar Khiwani. When I had first planned to bring out this print edition many years ago, they had all readily given their consent to include their work; I am grateful to them for this. We have lost too many poets in recent times, but their words continue to light the way.

A Thousand Gardenias Bloom

"Here comes the radiation,
Even though the fragrance of gardenias
Makes me want to live forever."
— *Michael Rothenberg*

In my country, where jasmines grow,
gardenias are special,
from a faraway land.
Their fragrance wafts
halfway across the world.

Solitary in their grandeur,
they lean towards the light
through morning sun and afternoon shade,
evergreen in expansive fields.

In my country, the air does not turn cold,
but I shivered from afar
when the snow turned grey,
and root rot chilled your being.
The earth heaved beneath
its blanket of ice
but I was elsewhere
and could not feel
its tremors deep beneath the skin.
I know you held on,
sturdy, as gardenias do,
until one final gust
ripped you from the stem.

I feel the cold now
and the petals have lost their sheen
but in this field of gardenias,
a hundred thousand flowers grow
and I know you are in them all,
spreading the light,
unfurling the fragrance
that wafts across the world.

Menka Shivdasani
Mumbai,
May 2024

FOREWORD

Michael Rothenberg

Menka Shivdasani and I first spoke about the possibility of an Anthology of Contemporary Indian Poetry for BigBridge online in the fall of 2013. I had been working in collaboration with Menka since the inception of the 100 Thousand Poets for Change movement, and watched her meticulous, professional and passionate development of the 100 Thousand Poets for Change program in Mumbai, and so I was confident in her ability to organize an anthology of this nature. And, of course, I had read her poetry, and I was impressed by her writing, the strength and passion of her words, and felt she would be attuned to seeking out the best work for an Anthology of Contemporary Indian Poetry.

Over the past 20 years of our existence online, BigBridge has offered anthologies of contemporary Moroccan, Mexican, Irish, Russian, Japanese, Nepali, and Tibetan poets, as well as anthologies on specific themes or studies such as our anthology of Greek Avant Garde

Poetry, a remarkable collection of spoken word poetry by women of Asia, and Perfiles de la Noche/ Profiles of Night, Women Poets of Venezuela (a bi-lingual anthology). So, planning for an Anthology of Contemporary Indian Poetry was right up our alley. These are ambitious editorial works that BigBridge has become known for, and they are always edited by guest editors who we believe know their stuff.

Over the past 20 years, BigBridge has always been, for me, a place to learn. A place to discover new poetry, learn about poetic traditions, movements, and tendencies around the world. I have always felt there was a shortage of accessible resources on poetry outside of USA. I have always believed that poets live in creative bubbles, isolated communities of art that need to be nurtured by discoveries outside the bubble. Poetry, for me, has always been about learning, discovery, experimentation and exchange. I knew nothing about Indian poetry except for Tagore. India has always been an unknown for me. So, I thought, if nothing else, this anthology compiled by Menka Shivdasani would be my personal primer for Contemporary Indian Poetry. And so, we set a publication date, and I was eager to learn from whatever Menka gathered for me and the BigBridge reader.

It is important, I think, to note that I have always told myself never to take the scope and depth of any BigBridge anthology or installation as the final word on a subject. Anthologies are, by their nature, limited. Who could know all of the poetry of a country as vast as India, a country with so great a tradition of literature? How could one ever propose to offer a definitive perspective? The best that anyone could do is begin the discussion and open the dialogue, to set the path for others, to make the way. In regard to these BigBridge anthologies, I have always understood that they are more like introductions to a topic rather than the summation of the topic.

There is a certain vanity that causes any editor to aspire and convince themselves that they have been definitive and have reflected the total limits of a particular gathering of work. It seemed to me that any anthology that promised to be definitive would likely be out of balance, serve an agenda and never speak for the whole, and would lack a certain democracy that is essential, in my opinion, to seeing the big picture of any poetry in any country or language, on any subject.

But humility and enthusiasm about the grand and rich scope of contemporary Indian poetry always informed the work that Menka Shivdasani sought to complete. She knew the work would never be complete and was always concerned about another great poet maybe being left out. Her anxiety about this was actually her strength. She understood the wealth and magnificence of Contemporary Indian Poetry and sought balance. She understood that this work of a contemporary anthology of Indian Poetry could never be completely done. And so, after the completion of the first BigBridge installation of a Contemporary Indian Poetry Anthology, Menka Shivdasani, in her insightful introduction, foretold the coming of a second installation. And indeed, a second installation followed.

And so it is a great honor to have been a host to the creation of Menka Shivdasani's magnificent and heartfelt Anthology of Contemporary Indian Poetry at BigBridge. As a result of the creation of two important installations at BigBridge, I have begun to learn in earnest. And it is now exciting to know that a new manifestation of this anthology will exist with the publication of a print version of the anthology, and I am not surprised that this print version will reflect an expansion of the work begun at BigBridge. Learning continues and grows, and more voices of great poets are revealed for anyone interested in knowing about the contemporary poetry of India. Thank you, Menka Shivdasani, for your dedication and perseverance in expanding our awareness of this important and vast world of beauty that is contemporary Indian poetry.

February 2018

Anthology of Contemporary
Indian Poetry I
(2013)

ADIL JUSSAWALLA

Poker-Faced

I am deceiving you. But think it is merely at cards.
Think love is excluded from hands we hold – apart –
As fate deals us. Think they are only discards,
Throwaway rags, that bring them together, while art
And skill (perversely) lie not in revealing my hand
But in bluffing it: in giving you what I label worthless
Play an unguessed at game, perfecting my hand;
Unsuspected, keep what I hold most precious.

Yes, love for each other is out of it. Since what we keep
To ourselves to grow to perfection we hold dearer
Then what we give, what love grows so dearly deep
As self-love? We kissed, you were nearer
My heart than its beat, but who did you see in my eyes?
Fool! Your King of Hearts has a double-edged sword
And a double face: the Joker laughs out his lies
Before my silent King of Death, my dark Lord.

I hold the whole court. Think I could have packed
The game before this, stung your pauper's cards
With my sovereign jacks of knowledge, stacked
Art against your ignorance ... It wasn't hard
To deceive you. But, as the one consummation
Of self-love is Death – my one self-perfecting.
Self-commanding Mentor – he'll force a conclusion
When he calls *his* card into play: the Black King
Who governs my life and my art.

I've told you now. We're quits and we must part.
Should you be waiting for me tomorrow
And I never come, pretend that I know
I'm in light; end of a game squarely packed in my heart
Where all ends and kings and pretences start.

A Bomb-site Seen from a Railway Bridge

As if the broken stumps were a girl's
Starved shoulders: as if the dusty rubble
Were her hair starfished across a pillow,
I would push my fingers through its grit.

I would press my bones into the bony
Shoulder of these scarred homes, as
I pass above their sardined tops, concealed:
Reach out and rasp and clean the greasy tin.

But children throwing stones, trenched behind mounds,
Holler and kill and crumple like stale newssheets
Unsatisfied with spotless skies of peace,
And I begin to count my enemies.

Violence is a culture found on playgrounds.
Cities fall to let their children breathe.

This poem first appeared in Land's End, under the title A Bomb-Site

Her Safe House

Mother
walking up a corridor
with a stick
as frail as
tissue paper
bunched
on a stick
moving up a corridor
inch by inch
a hairball
being pushed
by a breeze
into her safe house
her sonless kitchen.

From Trying to Say Goodbye, Almost Island Books, 2011

ARVIND KRISHNA MEHROTRA

Approaching Fifty

Sometimes,
In unwiped bathroom mirrors,
He sees all three faces
Looking at him:

His own,
The grey-haired man's
Whose life policy has matured,
And the mocking youth's
Who paid the first premium.

From *The Transfiguring Places*, **Ravi Dayal Publisher**

The Sale

I
It's yours for the price, and these
old bits have character too. Today
they may not be available.
Naturally I can't press you
to buy them, and were I not leaving
– you hear the sun choking with an eclipse –
I would never have thought of selling.
You may take your time though, and
satisfy yourself. Yes, this is Europe
that America. This scarecrow Asia
that groin Africa and amputated
Australia. These five. I don't have more.
Maybe another egg-laying island remains
in the sea. You remember in my letter
I wrote of forests? They're wrapped
in leaves and there should be
no trouble in carrying them.
This skull contains the rivers.
About that I'm sorry. Had you come
yesterday I might have given you two.
I'll take another look. Yes, I do
have a mummy somewhere; only last
night the pyramids came
and knocked at my gate for a long time.

II
Would you mind if I showed you
a few more things now yours?
Be careful, one river is still wet
and slippery; its waters continue to

run like footprints. Well, this is a
brick and we call that string.
This microscope contains the margins
of a poem. I've a map left, drawn
by migrating birds.
Come into the attic.
That's not a doll – it's the
photograph of a brain walking
on sand and in the next one
it's wearing an oasis-like crown,
I must also show you a tiger's skin
which once hid a palace.
On one roof you'll see
the antelope's horns
on another the falling wind. These round
things are bangles, that long one
a gun. This cave is the inside
of a boot. And here
carved wheels turn through stone.

III
I wish you had asked me earlier.
The paintings have been bought
by a broken mirror
but I think I can lead you
to a crack in the wall.
I've a skeleton too.
It's full of butterflies
who at dawn will carry away
the crown.
I've also a wheel-chair to show you;
it belonged to my uncle
and one day the hook

that hangs from the sky
touched him. If you open the
cupboard you'll see his memory
on the upper shelves and two books
now yours.
Ruskin's *Lectures on Art* and a
Short History of English Literature by Legouis.
I'll take another minute.
Can you climb this ladder?
Well, that's the sun and moon
and with this candle you can
work the clouds. I'm sorry I was
short of space
and had to pack the Great Bear
in this clock. Oh them,
let them not worry you.
They're only fishermen and king
who will sail soon as one's bait
is ready and the other's dominion.

From *Nine Enclosures*, Clearing House

EUNICE de SOUZA

Conversation Piece

My Portuguese-bred colleague
picked up a clay shivalingam
one day and said:
Is this an ashtray?
No, said the salesman.
This is our god.

Advice to Women

Keep cats
if you want to learn to cope with
the otherness of lovers.
Otherness is not always neglect—
Cats return to their litter trays
when they need to.
Don't cuss out of the window
at their enemies.
That stare of perpetual surprise
in those great green eyes
will teach you
to die alone.

From My Mother Feared Death

Alive or dead, mothers are troubling.
Mine came back and said, 'I'm lonely.'
I left the windows open and the lights on.
She was buried in blue.
It remained. Nothing else did.
Handed back to us in a plastic bag
her bones are forced into a niche.
'I'm lonely," she says.
I dream of her.
It's the best I can do.

GIEVE PATEL

How Do You Withstand, Body?

How do your withstand, body,
Destruction repeatedly
Aimed at you? Minutes,
Seconds, like gun reports
Tattoo you with holes.
Your area of five
By one is not
Room enough for
The fists, the blows;
All instruments itch
To make a hedgehog
Of your hide. It's your fate,
Poor slut: To walk compliantly
Before heroes! Offering
In your demolition
A besotted kind of love:
Dumb, discoloured,
Battered patches; meat-mouths
For monsters' kisses.

(**From** *How Do You Withstand, Body?*)

Post-Mortem

It is startling to see how swiftly
A man may be sliced
From chin to prick,
How easily the bones
He has felt whole
Under his chest
For a sixty, seventy years
May be snapped,
With what calm,
Liver, lung and heart
Be examined, the bowels
Noted for defect, the brain
For haemorrhage,
And all these insides
That have for a lifetime
Raged and strained to understand
Be dumped back into the body,
Now stitched to perfection,
Before announcing death
Due to an obscure reason.

From *Poems*

Squirrels in Washington

Squirrels in Washington come
Galloping at you on fours, then brake
To a halt a few feet away
And beg on hindquarters.
No one stones them,
And their fear is diminished.
They do halt, even so,
Some feet away, those few feet
The object of my wonder. Do I
Emit currents
At closer quarters? Are those
The few feet *I* would keep
From a tame tiger? Is there
A hierarchy, then, of distances,
That must be observed,
And non-observance would at once
Agglutinate all of Nature
Into a messy, inextricable mass?
Ah Daphne! Passing
From woman to foliage did she for a moment
Sense all vegetable sap as current
Of her own bloodstream, the green
Flooding into the red? And when
She achieved her final arboreal being,
Shed dewy tears each dawn
For that lost fleeting moment,
That hint of freedom,
In transit, between cage and cage?

From *Mirrored, Mirroring*

KEKI N. DARUWALLA

At War

we who are at war with ourselves,
our dreams moving along the barbed
contour of our angsts – the hit-or-miss
meteorites that turn space
into a shooting gallery,
flamingos that may never fly back
to the salt puddles of Kutch,
The Chinese spiriting away the Brahmaputra
in a gargantuan theft,
and India turning into a Bombay local,
asphyxiating in the smell of two billion armpits
and two billion groins –
isn't all this enough
to give us a collective cerebral bleed?

not forgetting our planet
which has a hot plate under its arse –
and my dream which saw
an Abu Dhabi dhow squatting on an iceberg
sailing down to Cochin –
haven't we enough on our plate
without having to think of war
and blood-stained *jehad*?

Filming

the screech of unseen tires
    sets the scene
the camera darts across a blinding curve
    at blinding speed
trees, hedges, cane-fields in the rear,
    even low-flying birds
        become a blur

this is black-and-white, the stripes ignite the earth
    grit flies at the lens;
the camera is a prowling tiger on the track
    of a blue bull
the camera is on track, closing in
on the dust-spurts from the hooves
    of the floundering blue bull

the stills come on now
    are we filming memory?
the stills come on now, trapped in the car
    doors caving in
the struggle, infinitely slow with seat belts that girdle you
    and jammed doors that wall you in

then low mist, slow mist, vapour-on-glass
    amnesia
and dreams floating in, mist-cloaked
    like well-disguised evasions

Defining a Sufi

It is difficult to define a Sufi
but I'll try. Always try.
Never say die!
(I am good at counselling myself, as you can see.
No one else would give a langur's bollocks
for my advisory dollops,
pardon the poor *angrezi*).

A Sufi is he who as he enters
a Bangladeshi fake tandoori eatery in Brixton
thinks he is in Moti Mahal or Khyber.
(He can't think of Bokhara as yet—
to think of Bokhara you have to be
spiritually very elevated.)

A Sufi is he
who as he downs one of our beers
with enough glycerine in it to embitter a jar of honey
thinks he is imbibing a Pint, mate,
at 'Fox-on-the Hill' in Camberwell.

A Sufi is he
who when he converses with long-haired Muzaffar Ali
thinks he has just spoken to al-Halaj.

A Sufi is he
who, as he watches someone suddenly stand up
and shout 'Haq! Haq!' in the heart of Cairo
falls at his feet, crying 'Master! Show me the Way!'
and when the master asks
'Do you have a match and a cigarette to light it with?'

replies 'you mean, Master,
'a cigarette and a match to light it with'?
and the master shakes his head and moves off
saying 'you'll never be a Sufi.'

A Sufi is he
who when he sees others
run away from a wolf
knows it is just an Alsatian
and moves forward to pat him.
(What happened to the Sufi later
is another story.)

A Sufi is he
who when his acolytes confuse
crucifixion with castration
admonishes gravely
'they are different.'

A Sufi is NOT he
who, when the hand of God
reaches out to bless him,
thinks it is Maradona's.

A Sufi never marches
with reality in line;
he is always a step ahead
or a step behind.

K. SATCHIDANANDAN

Burnt Poems

I am a half-burnt poem.
Yes, you guessed right,
a girl's love poem.

Girls' love poems have
seldom escaped fire:
father's fire, brother's fire,
even mother's, an heirloom.

Only some girls half-escape:
those half-charred ones
we call Sylvia Plath,
Anna Akhmatova
or Kamala Das.

Some girls, to escape fire,
hide their desire
under the veil of piety:
thus is born a Meera,
an Andal, a Mahadevi Akka.

Every nun is a burnt
love-poem, addressed to
the ever-young Jesus.

Rarely, very rarely,
one girl learns to
laugh at the world
with that tender affection

only women are capable of.
Then the world names her
Wislawa Szymborska.

Of course, Sappho:
she was saved only as
her love poems were
addressed to women.

(*Translated from Malayalam by the poet*)

Old Women

Old women do not fly on magic wands
or make obscure prophecies
from ominous forests.
They just sit on vacant park benches
in the quiet evenings
calling doves by their names
charming them with grains of maize.

Or, trembling like waves
they stand in endless queues in
government hospitals
or settle like sterile clouds
in post offices awaiting mail
from their sons abroad,
long ago dead.

They whisper like a drizzle
as they roam the streets
with a lost gaze as though
something they had thrown up
had never returned to earth.

They shiver like December nights
in their dreamless sleep
on shop verandahs.

There are swings still
in their half-blind eyes,
lilies and Christmases
in their failing memory.
There is one folktale

for each wrinkle on their skin.
Their drooping breasts
yet have milk enough to feed
three generations
who would never care for it.

All dawns pass
leaving them in the dark.
They do not fear death,
they died long ago.

Old women once
were continents.
They had deep woods in them,
lakes, mountains, volcanoes even,
even raging gulfs.
When the earth was in heat
they melted, shrank,
leaving only their maps.
You can fold them
and keep them handy:
who knows, they might help you find
your way home.

(Translated from the Malayalam by the poet)

The Fox

Fox is my name.
Dying of cunning.
Trapped in my own tricks.
Not wanted by the woods
Nor the village.
Hunted down from
Sunlight to moonlight.

First I discovered fire.
That grew wild and
Burnt down the forest.
Then I invented the wheel.
That turned into tanks and
Sowed death all over the earth.
Then I invented wings.
They turned into fighter-planes
and filled stars with darkness.
I invented war and spread
hatred among friends.
I sold arms to kin so that
They may fight one other.
As they fell, I came out
From behind flowers
Looking for blood.

Thickets no more hide me;
Nor valleys provide shelter.
Rivers refuse me water.
Sparrows nudge me and fly away.
Hares unite against me.
Forest-paths no more

Lead me to victory.
My howl of triumph
Is now a suppressed sob.
With my power I can
Now punish only myself.

O, Bodhisattwa,
Once you took my form;
Now teach me your simple ways.
Give my thoughts the voice of love.
Fill my begging bowl
With milk instead of blood.

Teach me, Bodhisattwa,
how to survive myself.

Translated from Malayalam by the poet. The fox was one of the forms that Buddha (Bodhisattwa) had taken in his passage to salvation through several births.

MALAY ROYCHOUDHURY

Chicken Roast

Puff your plume in anger and fight, cock, delight the
                        owner of knife
Smear sting with pollen and flap your wings
As I said: Twist both arms and force them stoop
Roll the rug and come down the terrace
                        after fragmented sleep
Shoe-boots – rifle – whirring bullets – shrieks –

The Aged undertrial in the next cell weeps
                        and wants to go home
Liberate me...Let me go...Let me go home...
On its egg in the throne, the gallinule doses
Asphyxiate in the dark.
Fight back, cock, die and fight, shout with the dumb.

Glass splinters on tongue – breast muscles quiver
Fishes open their gills and enfog water.
A piece of finger wrapped in pink paper
With eyes covered, someone wails in the jailhouse
                        I can't make out if man or woman.

Keep the eyelash on the left-hand palm –
                        and blow off with your breath
Fan out snake-hood in mist.
Cobra's abdomen shivers in the hiss of feminine urination
Deport to crematorium stuffing blood-oozing nose
                        in cottonwool
Shoes, brickbats and torn pantaloons litter streets.

I smear my feet with waves picked up from the stormy sea.
Those are the alphabets I drew on for letters.

(A translation of *Murgir Roast, from the original Bengali*)

Preparation

Who claims I'm ruined? Because I'm without
                         fangs and claws?
Are they necessary? How do you forget the knife
plunged in the abdomen up to the hilt?
                              Green cardamom leaves
for the buck, Art of hatred and anger
and of war, gagged and tied Santhal woman,
                       pink of lungs shattered
by a restless dagger?
Pride of sword pulled back from heart? I don't have
songs or music. Only shrieks, when the mouth is opened,
wordless odour of the jungle; corner of kin
                     and sin-sannyas.
Didn't pray for a tongue to take back the groans,
power to gnash and bear it. Fearless gunpowder bleats:
stupidity is the sole faith – maimed generosity –
I leap on the gambling table, knife in my teeth.
                              Encircle me,
rush in from tea and coffee plateaux
in your gumboots of pleasant wages
the way Jarasandha's genital is bisected
                           and diamonds glow.
The skill of beating up is the only wisdom.
In misery, I play the burglar's stick like a flute
brittle affection of the wax-skin apple
She-ants undress their wings
                 before copulating or death maybe.
I thump my thighs with alternate shrieks:
             Vacate the Universe.
Get out you omnicompetent
Conch-shell in scratching monkey-hand

lotus and mace and discus-blade.
Let there be salt-rebellion of your own saline sweat;
along the gunpowder, let the flint run towards explosion.
Marketeers of words daubed in darkness
in the midnight filled with young dog's grief
in the sick-noon of a grasshopper sunk in insecticide
I reappear to exhibit the charm of stiletto.

(A translation of *Prostuti*)

Throne of the Weevil

O ant-sucker tongue of the shy mammal
delighted in one-horned matrimony
terrestrial aqua and aerial
host-beast of smuggler moll
ruminant antelope
earth-roamer watercat the perfumed bitch
ate up sonorous blackhole and established
a slave kingdom in this ditch.

(Translation of *Ghunpokar Singhason*)

ANAMIKA

Without A Place

This is how the *shloka* goes —
women, nails and hair
once they've fallen
    just can't be put back,
    said our Sanskrit teacher.

Frozen in place out of fear
we girls held on tight to our seats.
Place, what is this 'place'?
We were shown our place
in the first grade.
We remembered our elementary school lessons.
    'Ram, get your book'
    'Radha, go and cook.
    'Radha, bring the broom,
    Clean your brother's room.'
    Once little Radha got up,
        'That's brother's room,
        and mine?'

Oh, little loony!
Girls are wind, the sun and the good earth.
They have no homes.

    "Those without a home,
    where do they belong?"

Which is the place from where we fall,
become clipped nails, fallen hair trapped in combs,

fit only to be swept away?
Houses left behind, paths left behind
people left behind
the questions chasing us, too left behind.
Leaving tradition behind,
now I feel I'm as out of context
as a short line
from a great classic
scribbled on a BA examination paper.
Now, we don't even want somebody to sit down
to pigeonhole it and nail it down
to a proper context,
Now, we enjoy being hummed
like an *abhang*,
unfinished.

Translated from the original Hindi by Arlene Zide and the poet

Mobile

*"Those who walk within confines are men,
those who walk beyond are saints."*

No confines for me, no confines
a closed fist is my boundary wall.

I can go wherever I want
but in this man's pocket

I can connect to anyone anywhere
but always under his thumb.

Even when he's dead asleep
he'll tuck me under his pillow
listening to the tick-tock-tick of his wristwatch.
The whole night through
quietly, I'll keep all his messages
coming from all over the world.

Those silent messages will glow
in my dark spaces
They'll glow like the cat's-eyes
of my dream-memories:
    Mother's ailments
    filed court cases
    all the office scuffles
    all the rush of unfinished kisses
    all the muffled calls
the faint quivers of many a held-in sob all flicker within me.
In me flutter the wounded wings of messenger-pigeons
each feather yanked out and flicked off one by one

once in a while, even a pat on the wing.
No matter how modern the world may be
the expression of love and hate are primordial.

I'm like the roads of old Baghdad
before the American bombings.
Parallel to the modern malls
are the old souks and the meena bazaar
glittering inside me
like archaeological ruins dotting the heart of the metro.

[Translated from Hindi by Arlene Zide and the poet]

RANDHIR KHARE

I Do Not Know You, City
(For Pune)

I do not know you, city,
You who grow as a wound does,
Edges dissolving –
Pouring into a grey pool,
Churned and set into slabs
Smothering heartbeats;
Eczema spreads burning the skin of fields
And forests that once smelt of seasons,
Pores sweating sewage;

I do not know you, city,
Appearing and disappearing
As you do –
In the eyes of the old, stiff kneed, in Tulsi Baugh
Stroking beads till they powder
Into grooves of palms;
Bells and calls to prayer halo their chanting;

I do not know you, city,
As you crawl in the shadow
Of a *dhangar's* horse
Down high roads of change
Searching for camp sites and grazing grounds
Signposts of the past
Now sprouting homes;
The ancient arteries of your heart
Clogged with forgetfulness.

I do not know you, city,
As I walk the serrated edges of your today,
Wondering who you are,
Who you were,
Are you alive or dead?
Is all I see and hear and touch and taste and smell —
Real?

Unknown Soldier
(In the crypt, St Paul's Cathedral)

He went down
In the killing fields of Mespot
Shredded by shrapnel,
Food for trench-rats;

In Nam he fell
Among paddy shoots
Beside a child
Clutching a wooden doll;

They didn't recognize him
In Gaza
When they scraped his remains
Off a dusty street;

He died again and again
In Colombo, Siachen, the Congo,
Rangoon, Moscow, Lebanon,
Lost among numbers.

He still leaves home
With a gun, a sickle,
Bow, arrow, spear
Or just bare hands – to war

For his family, his land,
Honour, glory, reward,
Living to die, dying to live,
His memory like ashes through a sieve.

Camilla
(In memory of my cousin Camilla, who drowned in the Arabian Sea)

You gave your heart to the sea one day, Camilla;
Heavy-thighed, broad-shouldered, heaving through
Flesh of waves you stroked your way –
Towards a warm red sun squatting on the skyline
Throbbing with dolphins,
Your lungs thrusting bubbles into the darkening air
Crying with evening birds;
You gave your heart to the sea one day, Camilla
And only your body returned, broken and cold;
Your void was filled with shells and weeds and brine,
Face down on the sand, you lay,
Exposed to unfamiliar eyes.

You gave your heart to the sea one day, Camilla
With the holy passion of a lover,
Wind singing in your ears the songs of the drowned
And the quiet lament of the living.

JEET THAYIL

Poem With Prediction

Because he's old and unsure,
he counts on your faith in images
and your fear, which is as pure
as when you were a child, turning the pages
of the illustrated books. He intones castrato
                              symbol & basso *portent*,
reveals the unexpurgated blood truth of fairy tales,
                       pretends
his closed, unchanged-in-2-millenia judgments
are improvised and no 5-star
disaster
awaited you. He gives you viral in exchange for Sister
Tree and calls it fair trade. You're allowed to whine
if you stay in key and watch your rhyme.
But your innocence
will be punished, this is a rule of the Great Gagadong.
Another is, You will love and obey him and let him lick
your wound with his infected tongue.
He brings you the good news – your tick
is erratic,
you are uninspired, dear
idiot, and no meaning will adhere
to you or your dead. His wide hand will rain
with blessings and good sense.
He'll translate the world into plain
language for you who are without ability.
                        Your need for money
is as banal as it is weak.

The real work
is his to accomplish – in a week.
Your demands are too many,
your skin too soft. You deserve the paddle of his
                                            handmade violin.

from **Premonition**
for Shakti

1.
Gone and *gone* doesn't mean a thing –
the world and we continue to be.
Happy to eat our pig and live, we sing
their names against the shame. We know
someone waits where the sky and sea
are tilted. She leans on light as on a floor.

The bridge between *is* and *was* descends
too soon, sweeps them up like chimney dust,
whose lips we loved, who were friends
when hands were hands that held us fast.
They reach to us, lost among the lost,
their shared minds stretched to the past,

inconsolable mouths slack with loss,
not able, not yet, to let go of us.
                with a first line by Sebastian Mathews

5.
To see if I'd still be here,
looking back at you, my figure
still, yours in motion, our
minds receding into the future,
the miles between us stretched like wire.
In my dream, it was a Sunday in summer
when you returned to the East River.
The city's last dogwood shivered
in the sun, but you didn't see her.
On the subway (your token had expired

years ago), you said, *Nothing's sadder
than this*. We found seats together.
I reached for you, but you weren't there.
Someone looked at me with pity and fear.
with a first line by Theresa Burns

8.
To our bodies, expanding, numberless, slow,
August brought new knowledge of rain
gone berserk, of water pouring south.
Our dwarf palm stood with her mouth
open, making her objections plain,
dreaming, like us, of somewhere to go,

somewhere safe from the sea come to live
among us. But the streets were gone,
taken by a color not-quite-green,
in which something unseen
waited to greet us. Even the sun
went under. It was time to leave,

but how could we outrun the weather?
Where could we go, and stay together?
with a first line by Elaine Sexton

9.
Forget the sea, let it fade.
How much longer can the craziness last?
    It'll stop
as soon as you imagine a new lost
    landscape
in which water and wind won't make a sound,
    Republic of the Not-Yet-Found,
a place you've seen before and where you've stayed.

Only forget the town's old
name, the taste of apples, the words you know
        as your own.
Someone new is coming through; you should go,
        not home,
not backwards, but out where the light is wide
      and those you lost are by your side,
radiant, ambulant, their downed bodies whole.

Everybody forgets every dear thing.
I know how it goes. This is safe keeping.
      with a first line by Curtis Bauer

10.
When it rains, the dead descend, you appear,
the smell of rainwater in your hair,

wearing the ring I placed on your finger,
a scent like heat and a voice not yours, a
child's voice singing of age-old danger,
in Hindi, a lover's lament from *Pyaasa*.

Your lips, clear of the color you wear,
are not new to me, are lovely and bare,

and our old argument still burns.
How soon will you forget me if I die?
By the river in this room and the way it returns,
I swear, If I forget you, let everything die.
When it rains the dead ascend, disappear
where we cannot follow, into the living air.
    with a first line by Michelle Yasmin Valladares

MANOHAR SHETTY

Elegy

One by one they fall away,
Some gently like brown leaves.
Others with gnarled roots
Hold fast to their
Bleak and emptied plot
To which no water or salt,
Prayer or miracle can
Grant another lease.
But sure as the turning days,
There will be other trees
Wet with rain and crowned
Green in the sun and other
Leaves born with new
Lines on their palms.

Animal Planet

Snakes driven from their homes
By blueprints and bulldozers
Will invade your own –
They're not mimicking parrots,
Prize-winning piglets, Olympian
Doves or postal pigeons.
They have minds of their own.

Tigers drummed out of their dens
Will go house-hunting
In your playgrounds.
They'll dine on a portion or two
In your cattle pen, their
Claws forks and spoons.

The snow leopard with his splendid coat
And the civet cat who wears
A most coveted scent
In a most intimate part
Have been invited too.

Arced cheetahs hunted
Out of your lives
By jeeps and searchlights
Are only exhibits
On your wall or carpet
Like those corkscrew
Antlers of the stag.
And the rhino still
Flounders in his swamp
For his stolen horn.

But lumbering elephants
Logging in at sunrise,
Caged monkeys, chained bears,
Leashed lions brought to heel
By circus whips,
And undercover beasts
You've never seen
Are biding their time
To join the team
And turn on you.

And some day soon
You'll dance to their tune.
Some day soon they'll
Make a meal of you.

Closure

Is not the fall of a curtain
And the players receding
Into real life oblivion.

Or the vicar dusting
His hands over a grave
And a rehearsed prayer.

Or smoke melting into fog
To the incantations of bald
Priests with caste marks.

Closure will not be distracted
By a wise old book or a poem
Or a piece of shared music.

Nor will it come by sworn
Claims of rebirth
And reincarnation.

Or from handsome
Donations to charity
And self-flagellations of guilt.

Or to a naked confession
To a shrink's steeple-fingered
Wisdom and prescription.

Closure is not a hired gun,
A bloodstained white flag,
Or a cloud of doves.

Closure is not an act of will.
Or a vision in cleansing sunlight
Filtering through mist.

It has no set doctrine
Or deadline
That says: *finis*, this is it.

Closure will come when you
Recognize it's only
A comforting word.

It will fall into place
When you accept its absence
Stays with you till the end.

HEMANT DIVATE

A Depressingly Monotonous Landscape
for Hiranya

i
How did the landscape in my mind
flow into my daughter's mind?

Right here in front of me is an expanse of
buildings, shopping malls, highways, factories and traffic
and if I tell her to sketch a landscape
she draws sunsets
a flowing river, trees, fields, shrines,
draws birds which look like scrawled numbers
in my tiny, overcast skies.

Never seen
from the seamless forest of this city
the sunset beyond the house in my mind
the river, trees, paths, temples, birds, footways
Yet how did these
stream into her mind?

ii
By the time she understands
this picture of my childhood
which has flowed away
and the answer
to *Why she draws exactly like this?*
will all the paintings by everyone in this world
have melted away? Or will they remain
trapped in their silence?

iii
Like me, she gets nightmares
of headless people carrying
the corpses of orphaned villages
into the cemeteries of cities
or ferrying frightful landscapes of cities
only to superimpose them on the erased villages.
The same, the very same landscape
encloses within itself
all the headless people
All, all cities have the same name
the same streets, same buildings, same shopping malls
all are transfixed in the same predefined places
like a regiment standing ready to march.

She moves along paths with
the same name, same colours
same smells, same forms
same faces as though clones of themselves
and at the same deceptive crossroads
she reaches the same statue.

No matter where she flees
the same statue confronts her again and again
and she arrives at the same landscapes
of the same cities
with no signs or landmarks to guide her.

In the same places
she sees the same people
speaking the same language
and with same shapes
same gestures

standing in queues of the same length
in the very same manner
going to the same stations
driving the same vehicles
at the same speed
in the same direction
at the same time
passing by the same trees
of the same height
of the same kind
separated in the same way
by the same dividers
on the same road.

The same people
are tattered
the same way
by the same bombs
and lie scattered the same way
petrified the same way
broken the same way.

In the same monotonous manner
on any channel on any TV
flash the same misery-multiplying pictures
monotonous
monotonal
monototal
totally monotonous
depressingly monotonous
totally depressing
dep-dep-depressing
She dips, dips and collapses

sees my same terrified, depressed face

at the last moment, when she lets go of
her tight grip on my hand in the crowd
and just like me
she too flows away into
the gigantic, self-destructive flood
of headless people.

I dream the very dream she is dreaming
at the same moment
I too see her petrified, depressed face
see the terror
and shudder
I forget to carry village to city and city to village
and reach here
reach where?

Something about This Shore for the Poet of the Shore Beyond
for Dilip Chitre

From the plateau of a raucous language
you kept pushing
the god of your gaunt letters

You didn't tire
In your innermost mind
you heaved

How sad
are the colours of vegetables
when their greenness is uprooted.
Colour doesn't remain colour
Only the tearful sobs of blue and dusky
proteins and carbohydrates are left.

You could pull so many tricks
from a Bombay duck's heart
you could make a tune
You could sound a whistle
from okra stew
From the pressure cooker's kicked-out steam
you would conjure up opium balls
From yourself you would make *abeer-gulal* appear.

You loved the yellow in green
the white in black
the sky blue in coppery
the crimson in blue
the carmine in purple

Hypnotic and free of colour, you'd meet
and lie deeply spread
like the Buddha
beyond the leisure of visits.

Holding language rhythmically you zipped away
Like the devotee Prahlad you nursed language
In the tongue of the deaf and the dumb
you wrote your Dravidian *purana*
wrote the song of the summit.
In the minute crevice of language
you thrust your chubby finger.

You are neither my granddad nor my great-granddad
neither father nor brother nor uncle nor some other kin
Measuring the shore-to-shore expanse up to this moment
why do you recline in my mind?

Are the Dyaneshwar and Tukaram resting on
                    your shoulders mine?
Is the primal *jagar* bubbling briskly on your forehead mine?
Mine is the darkness percolating through
the clouds of your flimsy vest
The flatulent doubt dangling from your
croaking, bloated stomach is known to me
I know the black brightness under
your unfathomable eyes
I am familiar with the sluggish
Bade Ghulam Ali Khan
who lived frolicking beneath your moustache.

Out of what bond did you share with me
the DNA struggling for a language?

Out of what relationship did you share
your secret encyclopaedia?

From beyond the shore of madness
why do you call only me by waving your hands?
Having reached the dead end why do you love me?
I'll get crushed under your loving shadow
I'll get trampled under your cries that come from
                                    beyond madness.

I don't want the feel of your cries
I don't want the endless tangles of your language
I don't want the secret god of your language
I don't want anything, anything from you
I'll see the end of my language in my language
I'll live or die
in the language even beyond my madness.

You took the liberty of
fondling the breasts of language
At times you touched her   straightaway violated her
Scandalized I watched your *futt* video
but didn't get engrossed
I too have experienced the genital beauty of language
and the forest spread over miles and miles
I am angry   angry with you   angry
You shared everything with me
but vanished silently
You went away quietly after reading your own poem
but didn't wait to listen to mine!
From **A Depressingly Monotonous Landscape** *translated from the Marathi by Sarabjeet Garcha*

TABISH KHAIR

Rumi and The Reed

Listen to the song of the reed flute:
It sings of separation.
Torn from the leaf-layered, wind-voiced
Banks of the pond,
It is joined to sorrow and joy
By a slender sound.
Who, asked Rumi, can understand
The reed's longing to return?
    Let its raw lips rest then;
    Let all words be brief then.

And I, O Believers, cried Rumi
(Having lost the man he loved),
I who am not of the East
Nor of the West, un-Christian,
Not Muslim or Jew, neither
Born of Adam nor Eve,
What can I love but the world itself,
What can I kiss but flesh?
    Let my raw lips rest then.
    Let all words be brief.

(First appeared in *Where Parallel Lines Meet***, Penguin, Delhi, 2000)**

South Delhi Murder

For three days she took it for spilled red ink
Or nail-polish. Then a scab of flies
Peeled to hint at the wounds shut
Behind that door. Her head buzzed
As she called the police. Such a sweet boy,
She later gasped to Mrs Guha, a little dense
But smiling and so-sweet, to think he bottled up
In himself the rage of 26 stabs, twen-tee-six,
You never can tell with these people, no, not ever.
To which Mrs Guha sadly shook her gold earrings.

The officer who turned up with two policemen
Also shook his head when told of the old couple
Who had lived in that flat with one serving boy
And presents from guilt-stricken sons in the US.
Having broken the door and located the crime,
He came out holding a large hanky to his nose,
Spat and asked, Nepali boy, no? Bihari *chokkra* ?
Some clues are so obvious they don't have to be pinned:
The incision of murder is always the outsider's choice,
Someone on the edge of life, driven by ghostly scalpels.

Sometime in the morphia of night when the roads of Delhi
Were white swathes of loneliness and smog, sometime
Three or more nights ago when the occasional truck's
Back lights faded to wavering bandages of yellow,
Sometime in a gauzed silence broken by yapping
Street dogs, so-sweet Shyam had crept to the locked
Front door and let his accomplices in. Steel rods
Had been used, and knives; the old man clubbed in bed,
His wife surgically stabbed later. A cousin was asked

By the officer to make an inventory of missing items.

Which was long: two TV sets, radio, Banarasi *saris*
All the inherited silver, jewellery, cash, in fact everything
Of value except the laptop, which had been left behind
In panic or ignorance of its value. Bihari *chokkras*,
Scoffed the officer, what do they know of computers,
Or alphabets, for that matter. It turned out that this time
The *chokkra* in question had been filmed, holding
Loaded trays in parties, and his address noted.
Justice was clinical, sweet Shyam nabbed in his village
With fifty rupees on him and a *sari* for his mother.

(First appeared in *Where Parallel Lines Meet***, Penguin, Delhi, 2000)**

Almost A Ghazal
For My Grandfather's Garden

A flock of sparrows leaves the *mehndi* bush like a shudder.
Two squirrels chase each other around the trunk of a *kathal*.

Herons stand stilted like village ancients beside the pool.
The soft coo of a pigeon betrays neither distance nor place.

Parrots squabble on the bare top branch of the spreading *gullar*.
Five orange trees hunch laden with unplucked and acrid fruit.

The pomegranate plant still retains a cracked, crowned *anár*.
Mango trees stand mute, lacking their summer voices of yellow.

The ladybird changes from spotted red to a whirr of wings.
Half-plates of dark mushroom jut from the fallen log.

Grass is an intricate network of roads travelled by black ants.
The earth below is a breathing skin, veined with dark roots.

A dry green shell is all that is left of the snail and his tracks.
Translucent wings are all that will remain of dragonflies.

Perhaps I should put my faith in the crow and the subversive rat.
A bunch of builders measure out lines and angles from a blueprint.

(First appeared in Where Parallel Lines Meet, Penguin, Delhi, 2000)

HOSHANG MERCHANT

My Sister Takes a Long Long Time to Die

It was the dark of winter
When the illness came like a thunderclap
They isolated an Indian girl in the Chicago snow
Hoping this Indian disease would go away
But it was America that had killed her
The sickness in us is named America
And the long long time of waiting does not die.

She had waited long in the dark of her lord
The lord she called father who never had a kind word
The lord who giveth and taketh away
(And now is the time of taking away)
The man she calls lord and manservant
The lover with fair hair and blue eyes
Who ferries her hither and thither like Charon.

My sister, she hangs by our slender thread that cannot snap
Because the long long time of waiting is never dead.

And she called Death as her brother
Brilliant, charismatic death
Death who loves and beguiles and kills
        but does not beget
Death the brother who no sister in life can wed
That unfulfilled love, that great longing that does not die
That long long time of waiting never dies.

And now in the brilliance of summer
of melting light and butterflies
She floats between dark and light
As on a river a swan doubly glides
One half flesh; one half shadow
Sister and brother / Reality and reflection on one river.

She has crossed life's flood on a reed
She awaits a boat now to ferry her to the other side
The long long wait she waits for all of us will never die...

Ashes of Gandhi
(for Ismat Mehdi)

(Invocation)

*Young man, in that May when to err meant
one was still alive, in that Indian May
which at least gave life fire*
            (adapted from Pasolini, "Ashes of Gramsci")

It isn't May-like, this impure air
which darkens the foreigners' dark
garden still more, then dazzles it

With blinding sunlight...this foam-
streaked sky above the other roof
terraces which in vast semicircles veil

the Mediterranean's curve and Liguria's cobalt
mountains...Inside the ancient walls
the autumnal October diffuses a deathly

peace, disquieting like our destinies,
and holds the world's dismay,
The finish of the decade that saw

the profound naïve struggle to make
life over collapse in ruins;
silence, humid, fruitless...

you, Father of the Nation, take me by your
thin hand, trembling like a brother-ascetic
sex-denying (dead, dead like us in this garden)

Belonging to the nation and belonging
to no one. The nation too belonging
to no one – despoiled

by the rich. And I reach out in the fetid Indian summer
from Pali Hill to the dirty tenements of Bombay
along the Parel rail tracks

sad in their squalor yet
alive with their Alexandrian sex
and hear the tintinnabulation

of the workshops of Trastevere
and Konya. The eye is attuned
to filth, the ear to music

As on your grave waves a strand
of sad homespun, left there
by some Italian virgin who became

an Indian widow: you take all
with you, the Hindu, as the dust stirs
amid the first big raindrops

on dry, dry earth: My *Arabian Nights* dreams!
Icarus could fall into the Tyherrian Sea
tonight; Indra descend again to walk

among the common folk
who doze like the autowallah
with swollen sex in his auto-rickshaw...

Morning is far away: With its salt-taste of defeated sex
and with the sad frenzy of orgasmic
animals who only know daily work

The workmen sleep on pavements
and the schismatics sharpen their knives
to cut again an already cut nation

As you sleep, you must know how
I loathe the bourgeois bomb I sing to
who stare and stare at me

As I sing, one of them, their history:
As one who knows them only too well
and you, your ashes I approach

Between hope and distrust
where the vast river melts into the sky
and crying out: Shelley!
And with patrician grace you sing:
      Lead kindly light....

One by one the lights go on
the green dome first lit   Lit my Parsi dread
we are in Harun-al-Rashid's Baghdad

And then with Damascene grace
which is not obscene, the young louts
plan night adventures conscienceless

as only the young can be. The neem weeps:
Everything is enveloped in the stench
of your blood and of poverty

(Epilogue from Pasolini)
'And I, who can only live in history,
Will I ever again be able to act with pure passion
When I know our history is over?'

Scent of Love

It is raining a small rain
A gentle rain over all the world
Gentle like that love which is so hard
To sustain or to receive or to reciprocate
Because men are greedy: They bite and tear

You from the mountains   I from the plains
I from the city   You from the forest
I a hunter   And you a deer
The city is full of the smell of my dear today

The musk mingles with the rain
Its scent spreads
This morning I lie in bed dreaming of you
I was to be hunter but I'm an inert deer

Sensing danger you wait
And I sense danger with you
Why is the world so crazed for venison?
I wonder at a living creature
Who must so eat a living creature!

And suddenly the wounded doe dies for you
She has dragged herself to you to die before you
Her stag
Did she not stay one night inert
When you slew her in bed
Just as tonight I wish to slay you?

Does not our passion only bring suffering
And do we all not die daily a little

Satisfying our longings?
Play go play though your scent drives me wild
And I have myself become wild in my love for a wild thing

Slay or be slain
And your hand will not be cleansed of blood ever again
The pain the pain of love is everywhere
And the scent of this musk cannot be washed even in a rain.

ANJU MAKHIJA

Pickling Season

Every summer, we laze under the mango tree
discussing unpatented recipes. When raw mangoes
drop on our head, we pause
to appreciate nature's bounty.
Then on to peeling, chopping, salting,
boiling, spicing, bottling...

Will the sorcery work?

By year's end, we hope, when
the pungent brine matures to its prime.
The zing depends on turmeric balancing the tamarind,
the chili complementing the *amchur**,
and if the asafoetida poured in candle light
late one night works for pickles
as it seldom does for couples, apart
since the first pickling season.

The alchemy has rarely bewitched,
jaggery sours, vinegar sears the tongue.
To change the recipe we've tried
with old ladies' advice,
but nature moves inexorably,
and life proceeds predictably

beneath the mango tree.

Amchur: mango powder

A Farmer's Ghost

Behind the trunk of a mango tree you were seen
vigilantly guarding rice fields; later,

collecting dung, rounding up cows,
you munched dry *rotis*, beat your daughter-in-law.

A farmer never leaves his land, they said,
till rice is safe from man and beast.

When bins are full, rice mixed with dry *neem*,
he will leave. The old man is dead, not asleep.

That night, I read about witty Veetal,
short-tempered Zhoting, man-eating Hadals

and other Konkan spirits in The Times. Next night:
ghostbusting, to dispel tales spreading like flames

in the night. Dark face, still as a scarecrow,
leaning against a haystack, you were seen

by all but me. Disconcerted then, now I see the point:
dispelling superstitions city folk like;

but, to believe the imagined to be true
can be a way of life, a fact, a truth.

SAMPURNA CHATTARJI

Where Do I Put This Love
for Calcutta, the city I left behind

Where do I put this love, this open need for gentleness?

Put it in a closed place.
Some place small,
like a little tin box, the kind you hid under the bed,
a tight, closed, small and secret space
hidden in a darkness bigger, darker, safer.
Some place closed and small,
like a fist, holding nothing more momentous
than a curl perhaps, a coin, a piece of chocolate quickly
melting, a vein, the place where lines cross,
put there by someone bigger, wiser, safer.
Some place warm and closed and small
like the O of your mouth, closing around a sticky red sweet,
a word you have just learnt, a breath
you have just taken and are holding,
for the time when you might feel bigger, stronger, safer.

Or put it out in the open.
By a window, perhaps, with branches in it,
and two nests, crows, a couple minding their own business,
their eggs waiting to hatch into the open.
In the living room, on the centre table,
next to the large glass bowl of cut flowers,
attracting no attention, invisible
next to that headiness, the smell
of wanting to be elsewhere in those flagrant petals,
back where they belong, somewhere out in the open.

The wide-open open, a field, a paddy field,
green from eye to sky, the sky a circle
around your thrown-back head, trying to see
behind, beyond the circumference of the earth,
the way the horizon curves and curves, closed and continuous
circling endlessly into the open.

Open or closed, it flutters,
heart, wing, eyelash, pulse, beat, tremor,
turning,
turning slowly inwards, outwards, onwards,
looking for sun, shade, sorrow, looking
for a place it might finally rest, contained
and uncontainable.

[From *Absent Muses*, Poetrywala, 2010]

No Shape Is More Constant
for Revathy Gopal (1947-2007)

No shape is more constant
than the breast.
Beast, wrest
from suckling mouths.
Wolf cub, dog dug,
mammary.
Tiresias,
see what your body can do.
Prophecies the shape of breasts.
The strawberry mark,
the brown aureole, the blue mole.
The man who woke up one morning
to find he was a giant breast.
Rest your tired head
before you go.

❑❑

Stone.
Under your fingers
the silent knob
of stone
grown out of flesh.
Feel against the breast bone
the crushing weight of
boulder,
Sisyphus,
cave whose mouth needs stopping,
groan.
Stoneman,

crushing sleeping head
with rock,
pass out of urban legend
into other lores of shock.

❏❏

Foetal,
centripetal,
fuge.
You were a marked woman
before you became a man.
Your nipples marked you out:
incipient woman, you,
until you went the other way.
Don't say you didn't get a chance.
On your chest
your commemorative breasts,
marking time
from forgotten days.

❏❏

Take my poisoned breast, little god.
The end is known to me.
So hard to play a demon
when you're a woman to begin with.
Bluer than poison, your lips,
harder than rock.
Break my hardened heart, little god.

Shifting, the planets are.
Cupolas of sky, minarets of rain.
Cupped between his hands,
right breast and left, each named,
like favourite dogs.
Dog dugs, wolf cubs.
Only a flesh wound.
A clean break.
Better gone than growing.
Cave at the mouth of the stone.
Cut off your breast, Amazon.
Get ready to draw your bow.

From *Absent Muses*, Poetrywala, 2010

TISHANI DOSHI

Cutting Broccoli

Between this moment and the next
there's always space for a lover's return,
though you may no longer weep for him,
or ache to lie down in the woods with him.

But say he chooses to appear on a Sunday
afternoon, when you're walking upstairs
for lunch; cutting broccoli into perfect spears
while the rice in the cooker is boiling.

Would you ask first that he strip away
the layers of the past, the times you washed
together in darkness between whispered words
and the husky calls of nightfall's birds.

Would you say how you've been waiting
for something to grow from the silence –
nothing phenomenal – just cracks of light
in the long doorways you've been walking through.

And now that he's here, do you let him
stand in the house like a new-born god,
carrying the empty weight of sky
in his eyes, saying nothing is irreversible.

Do you offer your impermanent body
against the solid frame of the kitchen door,
allow him to fall easily – into the future –
knowing the moment never disappears.

That Woman

That woman is here again.
She's found her way out
from under the stairs.
For centuries she's been weeping
a song about lost men,
the disappearance of beauty,
                            disgrace.
Now she's back in the world,
down by the traffic lights,
in the shade of trees,
hurrying to the parlour
to fix the crack in her face.

Don't become that woman,
my mother said.
By which she meant,
don't become that woman
who doesn't marry
or bear children.
That woman who spreads her legs,
who is beaten, who cannot hold
her grief or her drink.
Don't become that woman.

But that woman and I
have been moving together
                       for years,
like a pair of birds
skimming the water's surface,
always close to the soft
madness of coming undone;
the dark undersides of our bodies
indistinguishable
from our reflections.

Love Poem

Ultimately, we will lose each other.
to something. I would hope for grand
circumstance – death or disaster.
But it might not be that way at all.
It might be that you walk out
one morning after making love
to buy cigarettes, and never return,
or I fall in love with another man.
It might be a slow drift into indifference.
Either way, we'll have to learn
to bear the weight of the eventuality
that we will lose each other to something.
So why not begin now, while your head
rests like a perfect moon in my lap,
and the dogs on the beach are howling?
Why not reach for the seam in this South Indian
night and tear it, just a little, so the falling
can begin? Because later, when we cross
each other on the streets, and are forced
to look away, when we've thrown
the disregarded pieces of our togetherness
into bedroom drawers and the smell
of our bodies is disappearing like the sweet
decay of lilies – what will we call it,
when it's no longer love?

SUDEEP SEN

Bharatanatyam Dancer
for Leela Samson

Spaces in the electric air divide themselves
   in circular rhythms, as the slender
grace of your arms and bell-tied ankles
     describe a geometric topography, real, cosmic,
     one that once reverberated continually in
a prescribed courtyard of an ancient temple

in South India. As your eyelids flit and flirt, and
   match the subtle *abhinaya* in a flutter
of eye-lashes, the pupils create an
     unusual focus, a sight only ciliary muscles
     blessed and cloaked in celestial *kaajal*
could possibly enact.

The raw brightness of *kanjeevaram* silk, of
   your breath, and the nobility of antique silver
adorns you and your dance, reminding us of
     the treasure chest that is only
     half-exposed, disclosed just enough, barely –
for art in its purest form never reveals all.

Even after the arc-lights have long faded,
   the audience, now invisible, have stayed over.
Here, I can still see your pirouettes, frozen
     as time-lapse exposures, feel
     the murmuring shadow of an accompanist's
intricate *raag* in this theatre of darkness,

a darkness where oblique memories of my
   quiet Kalakshetra days filter,
matching your very own of another time,
   where darkness itself is sleeping light,
   light that merges, reshapes, and ignites,
dancing delicately in the half-light.

But it is this sacred darkness that endures,
   melting light with desire, desire that simmers
and sparks the radiance of your
   quiet femininity, as the female dancer
   now illuminates everything visible: clear,
poetic, passionate, and ice-pure.

Note: The line-end rhyme-scheme — a b a c c a ... d b d e e d ... f b f g g f ... — maps and mirrors the actual classical dance step-pattern and beat — ta dhin ta thaye thaye ta. Left-hand margin indentations match the same scheme and form.

*

Kargil

Ten years on, I came searching for
            war signs of the past
expecting remnants – magazine debris,
unexploded shells,
       shrapnels
             that mark bomb wounds.

I came looking for
                 ghosts –
people past, skeletons charred,
abandoned
           brick-wood-cement
             that once housed them.

I could only find whispers –
           whispers among the clamour
of a small town outpost
               in full throttle –
everyday chores
            sketching outward signs
         of normality and life.

In that bustle
           I spot war-lines of a decade ago,
though the storylines
           are kept buried, wrapped
in old newsprint.

There is order amid uneasiness –
           the muezzin's cry,
the monk's chant –
      baritones
        merging in their separateness.

At the bus station
        black coughs of exhaust
smoke-screens everything.
                The roads meet
and after the crossroad ritual
                        diverge,
skating along the undotted lines
                        of control.
A porous garland
        with cracked beads
adorns Tiger Hill.
        Beyond the mountains
                are dark memories,
and beyond them
        no one knows,
                and beyond them
no one wants to know.

Even the flight of birds
                that wing over their crests
don't know which feathers to down.
                Chameleon-like
they fly, tracing perfect parabolas.

I look up
        and calculate their exact arc
and find instead,   a flawed theorem.

* *Kargil* first appeared in *Platform, Yellow Nib Modern English Poetry by Indians* (Queen's University, Belfast), *Caravan, Australian Poetry Journal, Ladakh* (Tyrone Guthrie Centre / Gallerie), and *Fractals: New & Selected Poems | Translations 1980-2015* (London Magazine Editions, UK / Wing's Press, USA).

GAYATRI MAJUMDAR

Light Shift

My heart is the inside
of an empty blue fridge;
cold, white, and with
a low steady hum...
outside the night waits for
a certain something
not really sure for what...
maybe it strains to hear
a bird song, or open its eyes
to something uncurling and leaf...

Then there is the kettle
fuming, steaming, and gurgling,
and I think, is it over?

A brown cow across the road
outside the boundary wall
has been mooing all morning;
it is tied with a short rope
and can hardly move –
she craves fresh air and a mouthful of grass,
both in short supply around here.
Draw me within your long arms
and let me stay there
for the rest of the day.

My stuff still unpacked lies all about
this place – the TV on the floor
pushed against the wall;

and you know I still enter this room
from the creaking iron back door, not
able to access the main entrance yet.
The only constant in my life
is something I cannot put
in a box or into words;
this thing lugs me about
wherever *it* will.

Now the light from the laptop
makes patterns of blue and orange
on the wall opposite my bed,
CSNY sings "our house",
but all I can hear lying here beside you
is the silence in the light shift…

Tribute to Revolutionaries

I envy your courage, sisters;
you who have no voice chew bullets during your lunch break
(spit out pins of the grenades of your patience)
and I, mull, shake my head and nurse my broken years,
and am still unable to identify
the enemy. My words are deceptive,
they tighten the noose around my silence
and I spill the beans into this apple pie and ice creamed void.

Sisters, I salute you
and no matter how long it takes
I will wait until I look back at every wrong (with anger);
Sisters, let my admiration for you
protect you and your children from harm –
let the blood of your angels
color the square
in another red;
let the chanting (raze the prisons filled with the fearful
to the ground).

Where (how) do I begin? Where is the hammer,
the sickle – the tools I can work with tonight?
The only possession I have bears the number
of a soldier drafted in someone else's war;
I revolt, sign petitions, write slogans
but they have, some say, plans to bomb the bases
after the aerial recce; survey the air and water we breathe
and feed us leftovers of some superpower's gallantry.

Sisters, do not take shelter from the storms
that will rise and wreck the smirks off

those who stomp the waking hours of men
and women who wait and cannot hope;
who sleep in a 10x12, sharing it with 10 other men
(near New Delhi station for Rupees 500)
and others, who have no darn idea of how
words can empower (some of them can even read),
or to take the 9 am metro (or bicycle) to work.
You stand up to the dirty scoundrels, sisters; burst into light
(and a song) and reclaim the square for us,
                      us who have succumbed to
the morphine-induced painlessness (happiness, some say),
                      numb and unable
to shed this thick skin (or tears).
                I wait there with you (behind your eyes),
borrowing your strength and promise not to fail.

Outside the square, there is space
where all your tears will feed
a million stars.

My sisters, stand your ground, your water and fire.
We will shove out this thing blocking our view,
together; we need no guns, no arrows, no stones
to blow their cover and golden-chewed paper crowns.

(First published in *A Hudson View*)

ANNIE ZAIDI

Cine Sestina

Tell me how it's done, how these monsters of Lake
Desire are overcome. How do I discipline this blue bird
falling from my summer heart? Give me a shard
of your blood on a finger-long slab of glass smeared
with chemicals, so we might conclude this cinema
of who you are, and why I can belong to no-one else.

I have no faith in promised time, in someone else
wearing your face, your name drowning in a lake
of namesakes and lookalikes. This trite cinema
of roulette love and hearts cast like dice, of birds
coming home to roost – shove it! I will not smear
my bed with platitudinous dreams. There's not one shard

of truth about this being my darkest hour. With shards
of dawn in my eye, I come to you. You, no one else.
If you are not ready with coal, candles, almonds smeared
with honey; if our evenings are not crinkled from laking
around my district of genteel poverty; if we cannot be firebirds –
ashen, alive, legless, marking the holiest place in the cinema

of this planet; if we are not red, black, beaked like cinematic
creatures who always lose the last battle,
                splitting into a million shards
of a thing that cannot die; if we cannot stretch
                stolen time like birds'
wings and dust ourselves down with joy...
                Dear god! This if, or else!

This bone-tearing possibility of sheer curtains,
    a houseboat, a lake;
this glacier of longing sliding down a hundred feet a day;
    this smear

of want on my breath; this damning habit of
    prayer smearing
my agnostic soul; this scouring of God in temples as if
    I was a cinema
fool; this battering ram of hope on sensibly
    locked doors; this lake
of alligator dreams – Dear god! You think I'm precious.
    All shards
and shell-shock and chipped nail polish. But what else
can I bring except my worn talon care, my shorn bird's

body? Listen. I dreamt of the Mithi in flood, and blackbirds
trapped in your hair. My hands are birds, my lips are smeared
with ice, my legs are landslides, my eyes grey feathers, or else
a two-bigha farm where tragedy unfolds on a scale that
    only cinema
can bear to tell. I dream of turning on the shower and shards
of other people sluice my face. I dream of us, a boat, a lake.

There must be some place else to go – a safe misty slope
    where birds
can yank from earth, a lake, with nothing more than
molten lips. Here, smeared
with cinema light, we do not explain ourselves but are
    revealed, shard by shard.

City, Twilight

People have done these things before.
Heart sliced open, somebody has talked before
of ripping stars out of the sky. *What right has anything to shine
when her heart lies, mashed
pomegranate on dust?*

Somebody before now has wanted to raise a butcher's knife
and carve out the irascible sun
pluck out the heart of a planet
take a cleaver and make mince
of this thing that goes on making day
come what bloody may.

It leads her to think of all wish-I-coulds
why-can't-it-bes and she says (as others have, no doubt):
             *There, right there
is why it deserves to fall. The stars. The sun.
                       The bloody golden moon
that becomes whatever he likes and yet the universe allows him
to stay whole.*

In sheer surprise a star bursts
through the smog and falls
off its chair, laughing.

The moon muffles his mouth
on the nearest ragged cloud, swears
to show up – *same time, next month* – nonchalant, he leaves
with a wink.

All the stars blink,
dazed, just a little crazed by this charming yellow monster
of sliding loyalties.

The sun simply reddens his face, politely swerves
out of sight. He knows enough to show a shame
he doesn't deserve. He sinks.
On the promenade she pauses, willing it: *Go drown!*
she says.

And he does.

Against this uninterrupted view
(why do they cut the palms down?)
she feels the tide rising.   *This is madness*
she says
and picks up the phone.

Before now, somebody must have wanted
to hold down a pillow
on the gap-toothed face of morning.
Or hurl herself out of a seventh-floor window.
          She thinks: *This has happened before.*

On the way down, she too must spread her arms
in a final, token salaam to trust.
As if a just-met lover was there, waist to waist, arms aligned,
egging her on: *Take off your slippers. Fly. Go on.*

And she does.

She will not open her eyes too soon
nor look behind to see if the beloved follows this time.
There is no doubt this time.

Lifer Giving Advice to New Convict in Female Ward

Listen.
Prison holds the key to freedom.
Freedom is... what? A well-cooked meal that you don't
                    have to cook yourself. And soap.
Soap, yes, soap costs money you know. Which they don't
                    always give you.
You'll learn to steal, though. Don't worry. Steal both,
                    soap and money.
Money can be made right here.
Here! The coins pile up, see? Came from stuff I sold.
Sold cut-up bits of soap and bought a smoke.
Smoke a beedi, here... You'll learn to make do.

Do not worry.
Worry kills.

Kills you more than they kill you at home.

Home, *basti*, city, work...
Work, work, work, work!
Work in the kitchen. Work at work. Work at night.
Night's dark work... and here we are. Because once we
were worked to death.
Death's coming, this way or that.
That was all the choice you had – you, at his hands or...
Or he, at yours. Matter of time.

Time kills too you know. So do we.
We killed. I did. And so did you.
You did, didn't you? Just like time kills. Or work. Or men.

Men! The things they make us do!
Do you really want to go back?
Back to cleaning, cooking, pretending it's home?
Home, to that *basti*? All those cow-brain people?
People are horrible, you know. They won't let you be.

Be smart, like me. Sell half your soap.
Soap buys beedis. Ganja sometimes.

Sometimes, out in the yard, the sun slides down mellow,
mellow yellow sunshine down the front of your throat.
                              Think!
Think of not cooking three meals a day.
Days and days gliding by, light and slippery.
Slippery as oiled hair or soap.

Soap, yes. That's all you will need at first.
First time here? I know, you don't see it like this.
This is all you need, though. Trust me.
Trust me. I've been here a lifetime,
listen.

Arundhathi Subramaniam
5.46, Andheri Local

In the women's compartment
of a Bombay local
we search
for no personal epiphanies.
Like metal licked by relentless acetylene
we are welded –
dreams, disasters,
germs, destinies,
flesh and organza,
odours and ovaries.
A thousand-limbed
million-tongued, multi-spoused
Kali on wheels.

When I descend
I could choose
to dice carrots
or a lover.
I postpone the latter.

(From *Where I Live: New and Selected Poems*; Bloodaxe, UK, 2009)

The City and I
(*returning to Bombay after 26 November 2008*)

This time we didn't circle each other,
the city and I,
hackles raised,
fur bristling.

This time there was space
between us
and we weren't competing.

Space enough and more

for the nose-digging librarian
and her stainless steel tiffin box

for the Little Theatre peon
to read me endless Marathi poems
on rainy afternoons

for the woman on the 7.10 Bhayandar slow
with green combs in her hair
to say
and say again
He's coming to get me
He's coming.

This time
the city surged
towards me

mangy,
bruised-eyed,
non-vaccinated,

suddenly
mine.

(First published in *The Hindustan Times,* **2009)**

SHIKHANDIN

Cliffs Of Moher On Alien Lips

A vision is
calling. Lone woman held by Lir. Stone-faced Neptune
like things emerging
from the sea. And the sea
greedily taking in
the sun. The sun surrendering
every day at day's end. Not as liquid
fire, but as slush -
gold shavings of ice - crunchy
between conical teeth. Air circling with eagle
intent above cries
of riders
long past.
And then,
there is

You who have
never seen nor touched nor smelled nor held that earth.
That
earth standing eternally
free of hissing sinews. How
did you make that
leap, skittering down gull-clawed
rock faces? The scree spitting foam as cold
as dead fish. How
did you jag your heart on the fishing
nets cast out to the deep with bitter song lingering
above water as mist? How
did you
dare spirits

of rock
embracing waters?

When you are nothing
but a tropical butterfly. Fragile beneath the lash of steely
winds, skimming
over the words
of poets and playwrights, whose ink is
nectar, making you another
drugged-colonised alien on a sacrificial
stone turned bone dry with disuse. Carved
out from within you
will go. Though none has come
forward to bid you *Slan Abhaile*. You will go because
the name is
crouching
underneath
the skin of
your lips

Refusing to leave. They
whose shadows come from the songs of heroic deeds, and
the sadness
and the longing
and all the world's myths are here
already, and brimming
with the infection of their histories which flit above
skimming the distance of the haunting
line, turning your mind
to wool as it cries, "Who
were the tamers of the Name? Pray,
who?" And you with the veins that tug
and roar,
your
tongue
is taboo.

We Met For Beer And Metastasis

We brandished politics like scabbards
and impolite gossip like shields.
We took our chances like plums shaken down
from a generous, if untimely tree.

A blemished summer moon watched
the scum rims of our mugs.
A sly beast shadow-played
on the waiting road beyond.

Just a day before, a mate had dropped
down cold from our lives.
And we, fighting our fears,
were desperate to hide.

We hid from our own hearts
what our tongues were prying
open. While our teeth cauterized
our wounds with our lies.

We spent the evening tossing
around our ideas of heroism.
We poured macho sounding truisms
down each other›s gullets.

The factories were closed. Our pockets
were light. We knew we couldn't
give up without a fight. Even so, we
were mortified and afraid to return.

What can you say to faces devoid
of questions? Bread served
without complaint is worse than
a wound rubbed down with salt.

By unspoken agreement
We had gathered to drown our all.
The smell of youth clinging tight
to our boots and crusty overalls.

Hope was the beast watching
us from the far side
of the road. It knew we would rise
and go after its shaggy tail.

Not just for our downed mate, but also
for our destinies. Sunk into the dregs
that we tried so hard to read. Yes, we were
drunk. Our cups were brimming with belief.

Black Tar Road

at a certain stance
in the cusp of day
when rain has fazed stare of sun
black tar road bereft of men
speaks to no one

at a certain nook
in the arms of night
when rain has blunted blades of light
black tar road bereft of men
speaks to no one

at a certain pause
in the shy of dawn
with earth's heart beat in its breast
black tar road meditates
fire's retreat from men

retreat from sunlight
retreat from stoves
retreat from burnt egg and toast
black tar road remembers
earth's buried ghosts

burdened by the drudge of feet
burdened by the wheels
burdened by harried men
black tar road dreams
of the sun upon earth's breast

made from fire
torn from earth
fanning earth flames in its heart
black tar road seeks retreat
from the embers of men

PRIYA SARUKKAI CHABRIA

The Gathering Of Time – Dialogues With Kalidasa

Varsha

*"This season's rainy fingers puts leaves and blossoms on the forest...
slow-spreading low clouds sadden the hearts of lonely women."*
                                    Kalidasa, Rithusamharama

Rain

Once
there was no horizon.
Sky and earth mingled
in a womb of rain
as you entered me.

Now I lie alone.
My vision clear.
My body rich
with memories
of passing showers.

(First published in *Chandrabhaga, New Series, No. 12,* India, 2005)

Poems From Babylon And Persia
– in response to Tamil Sangam puram war poems

Salma, pi-dog of Baghdad, says:

Americans are kind.
They leave blood on the streets
    for us to lick,
    and morsels of human flesh

    stuck
    to charred clothing.

They return us to our ancestors:
Wolves.

Salma's friend, pi-dog Imrana replies:

You don't hear and see so well
ever since the bomb went off in the neighborhood
    dump where you had littered
    six pups,
    one-eyed, one-eared, scar- faced Salma.

Listen:
I've heard
the scene of feasting is shifting
    overseas
    and underground,
    in tunnels long and deep.
And that the bombers talk in a language

we can understand, so to speak.
I'd trot there myself for the spread
if it weren't that I lack
front feet.

(First published in *Soundings Issue 34, A journal of politics and culture*, **U K**, 2007)

Refuse/ Refused

Fragments From Three Cantos
1.
Hahaha, he laughs, the bald boy, veteran rag-picker sitting on a pile of junk, toes splayed.

Around him strays snarl or sleep, his pets, his messengers from the world outside, bound

to this dump by its bounty. There's nothing you can't find here, he laughs, this mini lord of

litter, here's a part of a ladder to dreams, a broken keyboard to miracles, a magic shoe

with a hole in its sole, a silken bra of torn desires, and mountains of bags and more bags that

leak their stink as joss sticks offered to me. The city's memories are strewn

at my feet like flowers of pus. So much waste and so much want like the cut-up girl

in that bag near the car parts, she's refuse now 'cause she refused to sleep with him.

This is my kingdom come, this is your kingdom come; come, don't refuse your part of it...

First published in *TRASH* Alphabet City – MIT Press, Canada, 2007.

JERRY PINTO

I Want a Poem

I want a poem like thick tropical rain
Dense green spatter of syllables
Drumbeat consonants, fertile with meaning.
Sudden. Short. Unforgettable.
Afterwards, jungle silence.

I want a poem like a Russian circus
You should know it has been trained.
No ordinary everyday poem could leap like that.
No quotidian poem could shimmer, spangle, exult like that.
Oh satin, yes, and yes, fakery, and then
Popcorn applause and a lonely child,
Big-eyed, dreaming of running away to the poem.

I want a poem like an animal.
You should be able to eat it. Or domesticate it.
You should be able to befriend it. Or behead it.
You could carry it around or make it bear your burdens.
You could, should, oh should, so should, clean up after it.
Afterwards: Skeleton poem rides in night terror through
          ice cream cloud cover.

I want a poem.
I want a poem.
I get instead this poem.
A poem of clanking wants like a pile of *bhaandi-bartan*
          going over a waterfall in a barrel.
A poem of whispering needs like a tree whose branches

scrape plea-bargains from the pavement as it is dragged to
the bonfire.
I want a poem
        like a chorus of angels,
        a chamber of horrors,
        a block buster film,
        a sexcapade with candlewax,
        an anaconda adventure,
        a ride in a Batmobile,
        a contessa in a fountain.
I want a poem.

Alt-Ctrl-Dlt

So easy to delete, backspace, or even
in extremis
Alt-Ctrl-Dlt all at once.

Alt
Against the parallel universes,
the parallel possibilities
the parallel lives.

Ctrl
The illusion
slips away
if you look at it
directly.

Dlt
Does not exist.

House Repairs

All it took was the flick of a chisel,
And the bathroom wall came sighing down.
It wasn't quite what we had hoped for
But we took it for what it was:
One more act
in a prolonged dramaturgy
of cement.

The new wall came up quickly.
Overnight, it was back in place
It was all that a new wall should be
Or so we hoped.

Only the next morning and the next
When, sleep-clogged, we lurched into it
We found it was our old wall.
With a suicide note still scrawled on it
With blood still fresh splashed on it.

We paid the masons anyway
And learned something about renovation.

MEENA KANDASAMY

Passion Becomes Piety

the guilt-glazed love lay on andal's breasts,
thick and heavy as him.

    frightened with force
and locked away, she conjured him every night.
her emperumaan, her emperor-man.

recklessness on speed-dial, she became
a rape romantic. he, a bodice ripper.

    their bootleg shadows
burst out with the sun. people pointed fingers
at parted curtains, a scandal of shape-shifters.

her hair undone, silver-grey lips, skipped meals,
and nightmares of a thousand elephants . . .

    she learned to nurse
every rumour like a love-bite. in her defence,
she said her darling was a deity.

they sent her packing to spend time with him
murder as marriage, execution as consummation.

    nothing survived them...
only her poems which celebrated those fucks
he doled out for her frantic devotion.

Six Hours of Chastity

The day dies abruptly.
Nalayani, most chaste of womankind,
Carries the basket-case of a husband
To his favourite prostitute's place.

She sits in a veranda of the brothel-home and
Someone who saunters there mistakes the devout
Wife to be a mistress of guilt, a woman of night.

She plays along, she pretends to this visiting stranger,
This wayfaring man, who suffers and seeks salvation
By day, but wants to buy a willing woman for the night.

The second seems as different, and as indifferent, and
As she acts out a whore, money is a matter of ritual,
Shining, it appears at her side. Enter the third man.

Spice vendor, smelling of sweat on cinnamon bark,
Six-fingered on each hand. A wife for every finger
On the right, a city to stop at, for fingers on the left.

The next is lean as a knife, he wears black. At eighteen
It is a rite of passage. He twists. He turns. He shuts
His eyes as he thinks he soars and spills. Exit the fourth.

To increase the number of his sins against recoiling skin,
To drown his sorrow and his loss, to fight the knaves
Who make him what he was, in walks the gambler.

"After the fifth man, every woman becomes a temple."
In the darkest hour before dawn, the

Enters her, to make love to her leftovers, fidgeting in his
Guilt, and cowardice, like the clinking of holy cymbals.
And the sun is born into the arms of a defiled night...

Six men, one for every hour of night.
A waiting angel, she picks up her husband,
(Who lies, clay-like and clumsy in his basket)
Not bothered to serve out spite or spew her hate.

Six men, one for every hour of night.
And on the way home, as his weight cuts her
Shoulder blades, she laughs and cries and laughs
Again, at the lightness of her burden, the end of fate.

LAKSMISREE BANERJEE

Haria

Haria is not allowed
to cross our threshold
or enter the thirty three million
doors of our gods.

He can hardly combat
deceit.

His dreamy eyes clouded, dark, are
folded and supplicant like
the green, timid under-creeper.

The brooms of cactus-life
help him to clean our dirt with
the breath of a hopeful vigilance
for a simple flash of instant salvation
with a lurking fear of a ruthless eternity
of god knows what,
never leaving his heart.

He sweeps our outside verandahs, porches,
the dusty pathways, the lavatories,
cleans our sullied bins and grimy cesspools,
frittering away his doomed hours
on the dim margins of hope
which never arrives.

Our Brahmin cook with
a noose of a sacred thread
around his neck,
pounds painful thunders on him
driving him away like a street dog.

Peahen Passions

To make my small point
I do not need to flirt with
Your fanned, oversized, ruffled,
Exotically anarchic, coloured feathers
On your empty crown.

My grace talks, walks,
States and remains stable with
My puny, almost invisible top-knot
Riding on a formidable foothold
Of regal infinitude.

The sense-blurring beauty
Of corn-strewn, dusty tracks,
The green aesthetics of
The torn foliage and mud around me
Make my statement.

The muffled hues of my world,
My dainty, wobbling gait
With a sureness of trodding
Despite the slime and dirt sucking me in,
Have an intensity, a conviction.

If you care to smoothen
Your great, chaotic headgear,
You may perhaps, still see
The revelling leaves in the storm,
Still feel the bliss of the pot-holed roads,
Or the laughing oysters merging in love
With the endless equity
Of the seas.

Gandhi at the Crossroads

He grew and grew like a huge banyan
with knotted roots
and a leafy shade
for us to sit under
and introspect.

He now stands at the crossroads
spectacled in stone,
piercing through the dimness
of truth
in iconic distance
in the labyrinths of history.

The vendor still fights
under the sun,
under the load
of his wares,
the slum dweller
still droops in death
inebriate in poverty,
the capitalist still
swoons in exultant vulgarity
bought from the sweat and blood
of the down-and-outs.

The Mahatma
in his statuesque immobility
carved in rocky apathy
at the traffic signal
remains forever forgotten
in the quagmire of life.

ANAND THAKORE

The Koh-i-Noor

*It was finally forwarded to Queen Victoria, arriving in time to
become the prize exhibit in the Great Exhibition of 1851.*
                        Bamber Gascoigne, *The Great Mughals*

Here, in this tower,
Bound by gold clamps to thin walls of gold,

I, who am pure mineral, neither mortal nor ghost,
Remain doomed to abide.

Of those who are sent here only the living escape.

I endure the doom of rock,
Inhabited by light and never at home –

No, never, never for a minute
Since I was taken from the stomach of this earth,

Except, perhaps, through the week I dreamed unguarded,
Unpraised and unpossessed,

In the waistcoat pocket of a British lieutenant
Who thought me worthless.

Most men who held me beheld only what I showed them,
And I saw much that their pride could not begin to see,

Though monarch and vassal alike,
Minion and minister, eunuch and page,

Cupbearer, concubine, courtesan and queen,
Only rarely guessed that I was watching.

I have seen too many blindings,

Too many tremblings of oil lamps
In mirrored paternal halls usurped by the young:

The banishment of music,
And the nervous weaving of recalcitrant cotton,

Where fountains had leaped and the peacock once danced;

Too many orgies, too much opium, and too much penitence,

Too many depraved flailings in the courtyards of mosques,

And self-assured mastectomies of prurient goddesses,
By incensed, believing hands,

To be moved or repulsed, intrigued or deceived.

These things I have seen, and seen myself too often now,
In the sculpted faces of mute attendants,

While ailing emperors fondled me in slumber,

Then woke before death,
Envious of my transparence, but unaware of my gaze,

Staring right through me with opiate eyes
Or eyes vermilion with wine.

I, who have never cared to be a seer,
Have seen these things,

And ask only now,
To be sheltered from the light that can never be mine.

Return me to the mines.
Carry me back to the dark that scorned me.

- **from** *Mughal Sequence*

Nineteen Forty-Two

August wounds him. His friends play games in which he
                                        does not join.
    His mother is a woman who lives in a cage.
    She is there for the Nation, his father tells him
– That man in brown with the big black keys must *be* the
                                            Nation –
He concludes, and aims a pebble at the jailor's groin.

The boy who casts this innocent stone is only seven;
    But soon he will befriend the frets of an old sitar,
    Urging the strings to embrace desertion,
Conjuring a lost void, till they are taut with images
He cannot bring himself to remember; or cry to be forgiven

For crimes he did not commit yet fears his own. The Mahatma
    He will come to view, with an awkward, half-tormented
    Reverence; and of course, he will be drunk often,
                                            proclaiming
In his drunkenness that Gandhi was a great man,
                                    though his followers
Were mostly fools–prisoners of a barren blinkered dogma

That numbed them to colour and made them believe the
                                    sacred flesh dirty –
    The use of Gujarati he will forbid amongst his sons –
    A coarse unmusical purely functional tongue
That Gandhi thought in, for Gandhi, though of course a
                                    great man,
Was wholly unmusical – and then, on an evening,
                                    approaching fifty,

He will call home for drinks his raucous bunch of ageing
                whiskey-swilling
    Peers; and they will talk of simpler days, when
                the streets were clearer,
Houses bigger, and the world more habitable,
                quaffing them down,
Till he produces out of his pocket, as a sort of joke, a
                miniature Union Jack
And a quizzically brown, fading photograph of a dead
                British king,

Crooning to himself, till everyone joins in, that surging
                drone of a song,
    That invokes an alien biblical God –
    And which they all remember standing up for
On schoolboy visits to the cinema, when films were only
                black and white –
Its cadences turgid, frozen almost, as the long

Last note billows out of the living room like a windy tent;
    And they drain their glasses in quick nostalgic gulps:
        All this, at two in the morning, while at the other end
Of the same long-corridored house, his mother, insomniac,
Knits little dolls for orphaned girls; or looks up from nascent

Amorphous snippets of Gujarati verse at a moonless street,
    Her husband awake beside her, up for her sake;
                both of them
        Too tone-deaf to recognize, or be briefly wounded
By the drunken anthem their son lifts in praise
Of an empire they waited so long to defeat.

                              - August 15th, 2006

HARISH NAMBIAR

Uncalled for

My ambition
never found a
watering hole;
or it would have died
the majestic death of
an Urdu poet
in the head of a
stupid acolyte.

Instead it died
on the Dadar platform
waiting for the Virar local.

Widows of Benares
(Based on a Henri Cartier Bresson photograph of the widows of Benares)

The calligraphy of silence
And concentric rings of water
Ebb and eddy, in
The black and white photograph
Of the widows of Benares.

Black and white
And no truth in between either,
Just a wash, a wash
Of moonlight; from
The unblinking bad eye
Of a sorrowful sky.

Like dimmer moons
The shaved heads catch
Their bit of light,
But one strains, and straining draws
With their wrinkles
Their deathwish on their cold faces;
The warmth of pyrewood.

The black and white picture
Also lies to me
Like a good reporter
Tells me no story; and coerces
My only story
Out of me. My widow
Is my mother.
No shaved head. No white

Saree. Not even a grand
Subject. For the art
Of black and white.
Just one more mother.

All art is another drug.
The shadow it casts
Into the dark, damp floor
Of my heart
Depends not on light,
But on the height of my threshold.

ABHA IYENGAR

The Way Out

Painting my face may help.
Strong lines of white,
yellow and red.
My body a deep purple.
He likes me scrubbed clean.
Every tiny morsel.

I could wear
a feather head-dress,
tomahawk in hand,
dance the Voodoo.
Throw some magic.
Bring the rain.
Pierce his heart.
Blood may taste fine.

They say a bear
licks a man's feet
and kills him with laughter.
I could become a bear.

First published in Up the Staircase, Issue 10, August 2010

Torn and Stitched

Torn and stitched. My heart or just
my pair of jeans, torn at the crotch.
It has to hurt.
Exposed as something naked, to be stitched again;
the world does not want to see
what I hold within.

I could throw them away,
let them go.
I have this one precious pair,
Lugged across the mountains
by a much-travelled hippie
who sold them to me for an exorbitant
fifty rupees, many moons ago

Jeans were precious then.
I wanted them. I washed the grime,
so
they did not smell of him;
went without a meal or two
to ensure the perfect fit.
My mother was astounded
at the cast-off jeans,
but I had made them mine. My cast-off heart
I have kept, have I not? Time and again,
worn it, winter, sunshine, rain, often ripped.

There is a desire for certain things.
My obsessions are peculiar to me,
So I have kept these jeans,
as I have my heart, special only to me.

I could not throw mine away
to get a new one beating in its place.

I just keep mine stitched.
Torn so many times,
So often ditched, or thrown.
Torn and stitched,
threadbare, yet my own.

I pull on my jeans, the crotch
I have stitched again.
The thread, though thick,
may break. I clutch my heart,
and feel it in its place.

Then it spills out
the blood from my mouth, and
as I fall, the jeans
give way, at that vulnerable spot.
Stitched and torn once more.
Till now I had the balls to carry on.
I, keeper of the old, the thrown and cast-off lot.

This is my last time with heartbreak.

Blood spills.
.
My fingers are not thread.
I am torn, unstitched, spilling red.

VIHANG A. NAIK

The Banyan City

To unearth the roots
of a banyan
is never easy.
Chop or hack. The old banyan
with the roots spread
over a century.

This aged city,
facing the withered glory,
now wrinkled, cracked,
weather-beaten,
with dim eyes,

has stood the time.
The heavy breath,

breathing. A river turns
into a gutter. There is humming
of vehicles. The city mumbles.

You grapple for meaning
in the traffic of noises.

The old banyan

is no more. You can no longer click
that tree at the crossroad, combing
the National Highway number eight

when you enter Vadodara.

The roots won't die.
You witness rebirth

in the mold of stone. A sculpted ghost.

SMITA AGARWAL

Transformations

" ... I can't live without books, ... "
      Jefferson
"There is no friend as loyal as a book."
      Ernest Hemingway

If air currents around tall Manhattan buildings
Can turn a discarded black plastic carrybag
Into a bird, gracefully gliding from one rooftop to another,
Somewhere down the line, swelling up to become
An overstuffed pillow, and then, an O
On the chalk-white blackboard of the sky,
About to burst, then pumped out of air,
Shrivelling fast like a punctured balloon,
Spiralling out of control like a doomed
Jetliner about to hit the ground,
Not quite getting there, having been given
Another lease of life by
A fresh burst of wind from the Bay:
If George M Cohan and Father Duffy,
While facing Times Square, can patiently bear,
Cup O Noodles smoking,
Budweiser, Barcode and Virgin
Crying themselves hoarse
Amidst the din of Broadway posters of Aida
And The Rocky Horror Show,
South Americans playing their music on pan pipes,
A black banging away on his Roland synth,
Yellow cabs, city tour buses, the M of MacDonald's

Next to the Visitor's Centre,
A couple quarrelling,
Someone picking trash off a can ...
If the entire face of a building
Screaming NASDAQ
Is actually a TV screen,
And air currents can make a discarded
Plastic carrybag preen like a prima donna,
Then why can't I be
As I wish to be,
In tired-out
Washington on all fours
Under the moral load
Of the Statue of Freedom,
Stern monuments ... mind-boggling museums ...
Why can't I be, as I'd rather be
On Capitol Hill, under Minerva's watchful gaze,
Wafted by gusts of Memory, Reason and Imagination
A sheaf of printed paper,
Bound in red leather,
Gold lettering on my spine,
Reclining on a warm-white-lighted
Desk, in the Reading Room,
... a book ...
From: *Mofussil Notebook. Poems of Small-town India*,
2011.

Angrezi Vangrezi*

It takes Roberto,
The stand-up from Vegas,
To enunciate how, we of
The subcontinent, speak English.
U-ls-ka instead of Alaska,
U-tt-va for Ottawa,
Baa-s for bass ...

In the grand atrium
Of the Island Princess
In the evening at 8pm,
When we are all headed for the dining hall,
Formally dressed for dinner,
He swoops down on me
To say, *Hey Lady!*
I know you're from India!
You speak English just the way they do
In The Best Exotic Marigold Hotel ...

We're good friends after this.
Well into the night, at karaoke time,
I croon Abba and the Carpenters
To the Americans
While they marvel and exclaim
At the Indian lady
Singing well...

For an entire week
On the cruise liner,
Like the notes of an unfamiliar octave,
I hear different registers

Of the
Same melody ...

From the Italian Captain of the ship
Announcing on the public address system
A sighting of whales on starboard,
To the Filipino waiters,
The Malaysian deck-hands,
The Columbian steward,
The Bangladeshi bar-tender,
The female Chinese service-staff
At the buffet...

All she has to say is,
This is pineapple stewed in sugar.
This is vanilla ice cream ...
All I hear is
A drawn-out low scream
Of high-pitched vowel sounds
And zees ...

Note
Angrezi Vangrezi – colloquial Hindi for English

K. SRILATA

Not in the Picture

I
Adoption agency file.
Her first photograph. The only one in the file.
Passport size. Taken at age eleven months.
Studio backdrop: faded orange and dust you can smell.
There is no prior story. Nothing before
the orange and the dust.
Except a thick sky of blankness.

"Why didn't they do more than follow procedure? Why
didn't they do more than stick a bottle of milk into her
tiny, seeking mouth? Why didn't they do more than wrap
a towel around her elfin thin body?"

I am greedy. I want something larger than orange and
dust. I want a sky with fluffy white clouds. I am greedy
for some infant cuteness. I want pictures of the day they
found her.
Glossy, flattering ones I can enlarge,
slide into albums,
design coffee mugs out of,
seal into her life and mine.
Didn't they have a bloody camera?
Now what will I tell her?

"What did I look like as a baby, amma?"
Why are there no photographs of me as a little baby, amma?"
"Maybe, they didn't have a camera, love. Or maybe they

did but someone dropped it and it shattered into a million
pieces."
"But they could have stuck it back together."
"That's not so easy!"
"Why didn't they simply get a new one, amma?"

II.
Five years ago. A new-found first cousin on my father's
side tells me about a photograph in his family album.
"We are all in it," he says, "Your parents and mine, my
sister, me, and you, with your cute, shining pate and no
hair. You had just come back from Tirupati, post-tonsure.
Must have been soon after your first birthday."

I want to see that photograph.
I don't want to see that photograph.
I will never see that photograph.
I am too busy burying the kernel of a father who has been
absent, loud and long, these last thirty-five years.

"I have often wondered," ventures my cousin, "what
became of my baby cousin with her Tirupati-tonsured
head. But now I know!"

III.
I am leafing through an old album. My mother isn't
home. The shock of a picture with one edge snipped
off. There's only two of us – me and my mother. A tiny
bit of someone's elbow. I know, without being told,
whose.

IV.

I am ten. My cousin's a year old. We are playing on the beach. My uncle produces a camera. I hurry into the frame. Greed again. "Let me get one of Arvind first," my uncle says. I step aside. Afterwards, I refuse to have my picture taken.

V.

My wedding. My mother, having raised me single-handedly, has hired a professional photographer. When the album arrives, we find she is not in any of the pictures.

VI.

"It is sharp as an ice pick,"
I tell a politely puzzled friend over dinner,
"this desire,
for certain photographs. If you are not watchful,
it can stab you through the heart".

A Big Elephant in My Room

There's this big elephant in my room
that I wasn't seeing,
though not for lack of trying
on his part.
They say
he's been waving
and waving
his over-sized trunk
in front of my face,
for decades now,
and has even lost a kilo or two
performing – for my sole benefit -
over a hundred and one circus acts.
But a Big-Elephant blindness
must have covered my eyes
like a film of cataract,
for I swear I never saw him.

Last evening, though,
when the fellow splashed
a trunk-full of water on my face,
I woke up to see the outline
of something large and grey,
tunnelling its elephantine way
slowly underground,
to the cold, dark place
where all Big Elephants are born.

ANUPAMA RAJU

Ganesha's Ghazal

There was a time I was the most popular god
Now I sit on walls as a redundant, ocular god.

They put me under chatty trees and gossiped
into my munificent ears. I was their jocular god.

I was Vigneshwara, the revered remover of obstacles
invoked in mother tongues: Me, their vernacular god.

Augusts carried me in frenzied parades. They were drunk.
Threw me in the ocean, drowned a former spectacular god.

Saffron gods rejoiced in victory over me. Summers
soured as they abandoned their canicular god.

I no longer digest divinity. A new diet and avatar suit me.
Made of metropolitan particles. Here is your molecular god.

Some hire me for special occasions – they're kind.
Found my occupation as a daily wage, non-stellar god.

I am the solitary Ganesha, sings an incomparable voice.
"Lost deaf elephant in a jungle of prayers – Not a god."

The Time-Eater

He eats time because his bones will need memories
when they are stripped of flesh.

He eats time because whenever he opens his mouth
yesterday's profanity turns into today's poetry.

He eats time because his body is a clock
waiting to fill someone's tomorrow.

He eats time because his days shrivel into ants
gathering around dead conversations.

He eats time because his nights grow into snakes
slinking through aging loves.

He eats time because he needs to breathe:
Against the past, before time eats him.

(This poem first appeared in The Caravan Magazine, November 2012, and later in Nine, Anupama Raju, Speaking Tiger Books, 2015)

MUSTANSIR DALVI

Why Someone Needed to Kick the Infant Kafka in the Balls

Every poet
wants to wake
as Gregor Samsa
one morning.

Every poet wants
to drag his belly in the dirt,
to be exalted by coarse burns
forming welts around his navel.

Every poet would
willingly put himself in harm's way
to be squished into concupiscent curd
by someone who doesn't even notice.

Prayer Can Change Your Fate, Too

Prayer can change your fate, too.
Have your problems
brought you down?
Here is some instant relief.

An open challenge.
Benefits shall be accrued
within twelve hours flat,
with full guarantee.

Every desire fulfilled,
one hundred percent.
[Jpeg Saibaba, saffron saturated,
right hand in *abhaya*]

Laxmi slips through fingers?
Make profit in business.
Be free of debt.
Succeed in employment.

Has someone
fed you something?
Made you drink something?
Is love betrayed?

Love marriage? Tie the knot
with the one you desire.
Domestic strife? Get the lot
out of the divorce.

Does that other woman
your man has taken

rob you of your sleep?
Be blessed with a manchild.

Alleviate court matters.
Find success in films.
Cut back on masturbation.
100%, immediate satisfaction.

Problems solved, A to Zee,
by Baba Amanjee Bangalee
(Jogeshwari East),
Enchantment Specialist.

RIZIO YOHANNAN RAJ

Digambara

I stand before the madman
listening to his laughter.
Amid the noises of the road,
it is a reminder

of your closed eyes,
your long arms,
your ruffled hair,
your forgetful ecstasy.

I no longer want
my mirror on the wall.
As in a clear drop of sun
I can see the world in its infancy:

clay-coloured, wide-eyed, pearl-like.

Daughter

I write this for you,
my daughter, who
is yet to be conceived.

Don't you for once think this act of mine
as either inventive, inspired by longing,
or just presumptuous. I only have a claim

of inheritance to this daring.
My father owns it: He'd created
my name before he knew who I was!

Our girl is special, it seems
he'd told my dumbstruck mother
at my naming ceremony.

Later, after the first of our many real fights,
his confident voice told me: *I made your name,
adding music to numbers.* He is an original.

Papa could afford such luxury
of faith. He spent his youth
in the age of ink-smeared love letters.

In my edited, ready-to-use times,
I have no use of his legacy of courage.
Yet, I improvise on his ways of living.

I have remodelled his limitless belief
in the promise of future: I talk to you, my daughter,
from beyond all chances of conception.

I think of you in abstinence, standing
at the farthest possible distance from you.
In absolute abandon, which is absolute restraint, too.

I must tell you of this paradox,
baby, before you make the choice
to pay me your visit:

I am split (as between my mother's *avial*
and my niece's bingo) between
loyalty and deception.

I have thrown away my priorities,
I hold no fond memories: You see,
I have a mutated heritage.

I have no surprise names for you.
And, what stories would I tell you,
as a mother to a daughter?

I have nearly forgotten my bitter gooseberries,
the long walks to school in the rain, and the stones
that stung my knees on countless falls.

I am one who tries to be here and also there;
one who refuses to remain framed on your wall
by growing thin and stout on a whim.

How would you like a mother, who dissuades you
from appearing at all, rather than count the days
to make your arrival possible?

It's not that I have given up on you, baby.
I am just scared of you being born
in my times afflicted by comfort.

To this painless world, I am afraid to bring you forth,
yet, if you choose to come to me, my brown girl,
I have a feeling that I shall die of happiness.

For, my daughter, you would give me a chance
to reclaim my primitive loves
from the debris of modernity.

TANYA MENDONSA

The Daughters of the Lie

Our ways are mild
but we have tigers in the blood.
We speak them smooth
but ice runs in our veins:

we would tear the heart out of an enemy
as easily as we would break bread
or pull a lettuce.

Nobody knows us,
the daughters of the lie.

At a sticking point,
the heath is as good a bed for us
as any sanctioned mattress.

With mercy to all
we have pity for none.

Although they lie with us
and stroke the sheepskin,
they never see the wolf.

The fangs and claws
are in the mind and heart,
and nobody is spared.

We have kestrel's eyes
and our kin are the wildness and the wet.

Come, the feast is spread.
You can sate yourself on us

and never taste our truth.

I Sing a Song of Goa

I sing a song of Goa:

Of the first liquid purl of birdsong that pulls
up the kingfisher day like a fishing line looping into water;
of the fist of the sun at noon and the cracking of the
                              parched earth;
of the brawling of buffaloes, breasting the woodsmoke,
heading for home.

I sing of the creak of the windlass and the clean
taste of water in the earthenware pitchers;
of the desultory conversations on the balcaos at dusk
– somebody's daughter; somebody's son –
as the crickets fiddle on hot stones and the sun dives,
dolphin-deep, into the sea;
of the anguished squeal of the Christmas pig, as flesh
becomes sorpotel on the laden tables of festivity.

I sing of the riches of May, when the mango and
                              the cashew apple
grow so heavy with desire that scent weds heat;
of the generous gulmohur, so reckless with its flowery
                              coinage that it
paves the country roads with red gold;
of the baptism of the first rains, when the round
earth grows hair: a tender fuzz of green on the skull,
over the bones of the beloved soil.

I sing of the knotted rosaries of families, that stretch to
                              lands far away;

of the crucifixion of weddings (nailed to the cross of
respectability);
of the benediction of funerals, and the village drunk
howling his loss to the young moon on her back...
loss of love?
of life?
never mind: it is the deepest sound a human being can make.

I sing the lament of the rape of the hillsides by bulldozers
and moneymen;
I sing along the veins of the rivers whose blood
is being poisoned by the excreta of factories;
I sing a farewell to the sons and the daughters who go abroad
to seek their fortunes, leaving the fields untilled.
This land is drenched in the voices of our ancestors.

They are stirring in their graves and questioning us in
their various voices:
will the bread we eat today be baked tomorrow?
will the fisherman's boat be capsized by the trawler?
will the farmers sowing rice be stacking cans in
supermarkets soon?

No one is safe, and every innocent must answer the charge.
The jury is out, and the sentence hangs fire:
all we have to tender as bail is the earth beneath
and the sky above:
neither is acceptable as surety.

But I still sing of the blessing of each dawn,
when we wake with the wafer of hope on our tongues.
The church and temple bells still ring, and the hoot
of the breadman on his bicycle echoes the rooster.

Some wake;

some sleep;

and some work to save this land
from the nightmares that gallop apace with our dreams.

If I sing a song of Goa,
will Goa someday sing a song of me?

If it does,
let it be from the throat of that wayside flower
that releases its sweetness
as it falls,
and has a stain of vermilion at its heart, so that the foot
that treads on it imprints its fragrance on the tender
hollow of the instep,

to perfume the road ahead,

until all the roads seem to be singing.

MENKA SHIVDASANI

Why Rabbits Never Sleep

Lettuce is Nature's sedative, I read somewhere,
so at three a.m., I finally
decided to make a little salad.
There were cockroaches in the refrigerator
but I washed the vegetable well, then peeled
layer after layer, startling a sleepy worm
that had crawled indignantly from beneath the leaves.
But the pieces lay untidily, splashed across the plate,
like splotches of sun on the street;
so I tried another strategy – common, really,
any housewife-poet will know it.

I took a knife, its blade seductive in the dark,
and I chopped. The fragments, I noticed, as I yawned,
had begun to take the most extraordinary shapes.
Somewhere I recognised a bride,
her toenails turned to ash,
a mother-in-law and husband shut the door.
Another piece bore the face of a politician;
a third was a child with eyes wide open.
And why did the dish resemble
a wounded Hiroshima?

I went at it like the smiling Nazi
in a half-remembered film, who invited
his prisoner to lunch, then demonstrated
the art of cutting carrots.

"Chop, chop," he said, and as the slices fell,
still smiling, hacked the prisoner's finger off,
two actually, with the words, "Chop, chop,"
and another smile.

That night, I discovered the reason
rabbits never seem to sleep.

Tea Party

When you and I were about to break
there was no question of a fight
over who would take the cups
and who the saucers.

You spilled over with steam,
meniscus rippling with the slightest
touch; I, supine on the floor,
licked the milk once meant
for you. Both of us
were china at that point.

One of us had been to China too,
known the meaning of porcelain freedoms,
sniffed red guards. One of us
had known the sound of an alien tongue,
harsh and guttural as it came
from smiling mouths.

Our smiles were circular, yours and mine,
yours from the top of the tea
and mine below - two halves joined
together on separate rims. When we blew
at each other, the crockery
stayed firm, and who but you
and I would know the liquid moved?

No, there was no fight
over chipped white glass.
The pieces lay upon the kitchen floor.

And I - I've moved to tea parties
in other living rooms, balancing
alien porcelain on a frigid palm.

Anthology of Contemporary Indian Poetry II
(2015)

ABHAY K

Chitwan

A river full of crocs
a canoe filled with dreams
—rowing.

Eerie silence in the jungle
an elephant riding a human
—trees strolling.

Statue of a frail man
at the central square
—in the city of rhinos.

Nagarkot

Couples
joyous—
almost levitating

an ancient watch-tower
stands still
—envious.

Bandipur

An old ghostly street
at the city centre

red brick *Newar* houses,
veils of creepers,

ever waiting for guests,
look quietly at flowing *Marsyangdi*

A cafe, a shop
Siddha caves at a distance

A trek to *Ramkot*
and a temple

to see.
That's all that's left of me.

ANITA NAIR

In Which A Small Gesture Becomes Epic

I have a husband.
Actually I have five.
It so happened that,
One of them
Strung a bow, and shot a fish,
Swimming on a tree
Through its eye.
He didn't look at all.
Except in a pool that shimmered.
They took me home.
A hovel for a princess.
I said nothing.
For love is like that.
It makes idiots of us women,
And I was just a girl.

Tall, strong,
Seeds brimming their sacs.
But such mother's boys through and through.
She had trained them well.
To heed and never proceed,
Until she said so. Bloody cow!
She sat within, their mother,
What secret thoughts?
What hidden truths?
What furrowed her brow?
Divide it between all of you,

She said as if I were an effing hen!
Wings for one, breast for another,
Legs for one, neck for the other,
And a wishbone to tug on.

I have a husband.
Actually five.
But all of this you already know.
But now that,
I am to be stripped bare,
Let me tell you,
About them and men.
For you can't not,
Understand men a little,
When you have had five to handle.
No, don't glare at me,
You bloody cow.
This is some of your doing.
You brought up good sons,
But not necessarily good men.

As for you, Dushasana, you mega moron,
Let me save you the trouble.
Let me peel away these layers on my own.
This one is Yudhisthira.
The wise one. Son of Dharma.
Untainted, uncorrupt, forever right.
The gentle tyrant rapping my knuckles:
Draupadi this doesn't befit you.
A father teaching me how to be.
You look away now, you coward.
You do not want to get involved.
Righteousness made you smug.

Righteousness makes you effing selfish.
I still have four husbands.
Which one of you will be there for me?

Bheema, son of Vayu
The wolf-bellied wielder of the mace.
You were the bumbling brother,
Seeking to protect me from bee and behemoth.
Yearning to fulfil my whimsies.
I see you wanting to rush to me.
I see Dharma lay his hand on your knee.
I see you second husband fall back.
Arjuna, my Arjuna
Son of Indra, my god among men.
Lover who feasted on my lips.
You were the nectar I would
never tire of.
You won my hand, and now
You forsake me with equal effortless ease.
So I am now left with two husbands.

Nakula, my radiant dark husband.
More handsome than any man living.
Horse whisperer, tender lover.
The younger man who made me laugh.
In you, I saw the bloom of a toyboy,
All muscles, testosterone and charm
But where are you now Nakula?
Or your twin Sahadeva?
The all-knowing but bashful one.
So much a child who needed me,
To show him how to be a man.
When you ate your father's flesh you knew,

And yet you allowed this to happen.
That I cannot forgive, Sahadeva.
So here I stand:

Shorn of husbands and all I was
My name is Yagnaseni
I was born of fire
Your scorching gaze doesn't shame me.
With the blue lotus
My fragrance is freedom
You can smell a Yojana away.
I was Krishna's Sakhi
But even that epithet I forsake
For I cannot be what you want me to be anymore.
I open my hair so you know.
I erase the marks, so you know,
That I am a woman first.
A woman through and through.
And everything only thereafter.

How Men Eat

I watch men eat;
The opening of the mouth,
The curling of the tongue,
The pouching of the cheek.
I watch how they slice and spear,
How they chew and swallow.
I watch how men
Forget to pretend
With food on their plate.
All I need to know about a man,
I find as he eats.

Watch the man who picks
At his food as if it were ridden
With hundreds and thousands
Of rapacious weevils.
Each seeking to chew into him.
Daubing and probing,
He litters the rim with suspicion.
This is one you could befriend,
But must never love.
For fear holds him back. In life,
there is none more important than him.

The man there who shovels in
With gusto and relish
Each mouthful of what you lay before him.
Life to him is a marrow bone,
To suck and suck.
Till dark flesh slides down his throat.
Keep him only for a while.

For even as he glows with all he devours,
Soon he will pick every shred
Of your life and thought,
Licking you clean of your very being.

Now of this one be wary.
He eats as if to eat
Is an act of faith.
Yet the plate is wiped clean.
Now watch as he trashes –
The cook, the cauldron and the stove.
Malcontent and miserable,
The food is ashes in his belly.
Everything to him is an affront,
A failure to measure up.
And so will you. Eventually.

There is the careful eater.
Taking only as much,
As he knows is possible.
Nibbling, savouring, never rushing.
The deliberate boy,
Who arranges his plate,
As if it were his tomorrow.
Everything in its place.
Marry him to your daughter.
For he will love as he eats.
Carefully. But for yourself, is that what you want?

Often I would wonder,
If there would ever be one
In whom lives a hunger?
To know food as more than food.

So each meal is for him,
As it is to me:
The last meal on earth.
To savour and relish.
Would there be such a one?
With an insatiable appetite?
For love? For life? For more than what we can see.

Wait, I see a man there.
Whose hand seeks his mouth,
With no thought, no joy.
Just another thing to do.
What monsters lurk within?
What bleakness blears the edges?
Then I see him reach
For a plump purple fig.
I see the mask of indifference split.
I see the hunger for the sap, the flesh.
The yearning to feast on all there is.

What makes him hide
His hunger for what could be his?
Is it food he fears
Or is it what love could be?
I see then the furtive greedy grasp.
The northern lights of desire.
The fig sets ablaze in him.
I could teach him to eat.
As to love I think.
He will teach me to see, I think.
He will teach me to be, I think.

ANJALI PUROHIT

The Wave

She knows she will break
and yet
she rushes to meet him,
the rock.

Rising and falling
a song
gathering momentum
smiling surf
rushing to throw herself
at the rock.

He just waits
patiently watching
her insanity
as she smashes into him

Inevitably
breaking herself into
infinite particles
spray and foam

covers him
for a moment too brief,
holds him
in her temporality

he just waits
patiently watching

her madness
unmoved, knowing

that even after
she scatters
herself with abandon and
abates, subsides, silent

going back into
her mother's womb
again
one with the deep

that she goes only
to gather strength
build up and
come rushing back

to be splintered
around him.
Patiently waiting
The rock.

Over and over forever,
she knows she will break
and yet
she rushes.

The Wave Answers

Yes, I know I will break
yet I rush
to meet him
the rock
patiently waiting.

Yes, I will throw
myself at him
shatter around him
into a million pieces
happily and willingly.

Fool, can't you see?
that every time
I crash
I carry away a part of him
with me forever.

All mine and
mine alone.
He knows it too
and so he waits
patiently watching.

He wants it too
to be carried away
by me
slowly but surely
and inevitably.

Fool, she laughed,

you will not know
till you wreck yourself
that you become whole
by breaking

That you win everything
by losing all
become one
by splintering.

Fool, she laughed
you will not know
the game
till you play it.

Shades of Grey

She doesn't paint pretty pictures anymore
Nor string words into merry verse
No, not anymore.
To be honest
She does try.

On a bright sunny day
She pulls out a bright sunny canvas
Stands it up
On an expectant easel.

A palette full with vibrant colours.
Crimson, ultramarine, chrome and emerald
Place themselves extravagantly
Light and dark
Tint, hue and shade
Sparkling, laughing and playing.

Carefree
Like lazy, happy school days
Recklessly squandered
All the more enchanted
For their prodigal profligacy.

And just as she begins
To steep herself in colour
An insidious grey
Creeps up from behind.

And dribbles down in rivulets
Of so many shades of grey.

Dove, steel, silver, taupe
Graphite, charcoal and stone.

Awash from end to end.
In myriad shades, to be fair
Some light, others dark
But nevertheless, just grey.

Like a brilliant sunset
In its final flush
Is so swiftly erased
Overcome
In the descending grey of a leaden cloud
Heavy with rain.

Before it can move away the sun sinks
Taking its brilliant colours
Along with it
Into the sea
Beyond the horizon.
Out of sight.
The sky left only with
So many shades of grey.

And the rain
It mercifully descends
In heavy curtains
Of hazy silver
The cloud, the sea, the sun
Me and you
Blurred lines
And between us
A million shades of grey.

ANNA SUJATHA MATHAI

Light
'He who seeks light must learn to walk in the dark.' –
St. John of the Cross.

When I was seventeen
And dreaming of distant lands
And faraway loves,
My grandmother said
'Get her married
    before the light
        goes out of her face.'
The light in a woman's face
Should not be so brief.
It's meant to last a long time,
Nourished by the soul.
Well, they got me married,
    and
        put out that light.
But I learned to live in candle-light
When the other lights went out.
One learns by subtle contact to reach
Electricity at most mysterious levels.
Light goes from the face, but
Survival lends one light
        that shines most brightly.
She who seeks light,
Must learn to walk in the darkness
On her own road.

A Small Death – A Small Joy

A small death is
whirling
in my mind.
A Sufi dervish dancing,
wildly beating drums,
my heart's manic hurricane.
A small joy came
circling into my
      sphere.
Seized upon, it soon
      took me over.
Small death, immense birth,
      life's foetus, perfectly moving
to its absolution.

BARNALI RAY SHUKLA

Palash and the Padmini

The valley stands bare-shouldered,
a hint of mist softens the gnarled
carcass of the Fiat *Padmini* BRY 1709
and the claiming fire.

The flames leap to the sky
like blossoms of that tree,
Butea monosperma
as Palash would have called it

looking out of the window,
bare-shouldered with sinews
like the ash-grey tree. His
words stay awake in Latin,

inflammable silences, in the
bliss of our union. Palash
lights up the dark. Flame of
the forest, upright, unyielding, stark.

A pair of headlights sweeps the
darkness away, the ambulance
arrives late. Men in white find
a tapering pulse in him — and I

hold on to a tiny beating heart,
growing inside me. A surge of
pain tugs at my womb. The
waters break to douse the fire

and wipe away the salt from
my kohl-tattooed cheeks.
Help now is at arms' length
in the safety of scalpels

the bite of the metal can't
bury the voices. Someone
whispers, a power claimed him
Another calls it...sabotage

A cynic calls it suicide.
Of course, most speak of
destiny. I wait for those
fingerprints on the bloodied

sickle that was found
right next to our
                    Fiat Padmini.

DEEPANKAR KHIWANI

Who Knows

Who knows what a talent can conjure up
Under the influence of leaves picked from the fields
Where men listen to the music of Kalshnikovs and thin lips

Yellow paint and a cornfield, a pale girl with beads and featherlets
around her neck and a tweed skirt sells to me the angle, the light,
a way of looking. Who knows what disappears in an angle

of looking where the locusts overhead drop nihilus rex
Someone somewhere is always dying, who knows
What the miracle of not being in the throes of death or birth

Can do to all is peace now. The homeless boy in Rio running
Blurs as he knocks again my television screen, replaced by
                a Cheetos ad
And on my page I tell him to go home, I've had enough

Of my lessons of the Nile, of Frederick the Second, of
                Marilyn and Jack
And Dawkins and Spenser still saying,
                Thy need is greater than mine,
Greater, greater, I sit on a white couch
                with bougainvillea outside

Reading of how the price of rice has doubled in six months,
and a Georges de la Tour has sold for 25 million,
                and five thousand more troops

have arrived in Basra, this great interchange we all are,

of the antique knowledge and indifference,
                             who knows what may come
of looking out, indifferent, on a clear day, I type, the type,
stationed with a cigarette, unsure, who knows.

The Vampire of the Underground

You caught my glance, as I got on, alone.
I looked at your shy eyes and shyly looked away. Bait.
I knew your smile completely. On the escalator,
I turned to see you, and a poem peeling off the walls.

It is a careful trap to lay, love. October, Melancholy.
Over coffee at a Costa's, steam, and your eyes beyond.
Don't talk to me of love, I said, because I knew
                              you wouldn't listen.
On the Northern line, the Friday, your knees touched
                              mine at last.

Ah. it takes long learning, skill and knowledge of love
to be cruel quite precisely. Your tongue
snared, your eyes shut, your arms pinned down
by the longing you could never hope to unlearn.

When I bit into your neck at the sort-of end, and saw,
disentangling my trapped arms, you heavy on the bed,
no weight on me at all, I laughed at our helplessness.
But, as always (and I swear it), I wept to taste your blood.

DION D'SOUZA

Angulimala

There came a point
where he could no longer count
their fingers on the fingers of his own hands.
He beamed with pride, satisfied.

Angulimala.
a garland/necklace of sliced fingers.
Some people collect stamps, rare books, vintage records, cars;
here was a brigand with a bizarre fondness for bodily souvenirs.

What prodded this mania to maim? Was it indeed a pupil's
abject devotion to his master, the envy of others
that tricked him into attacking travellers, numb
in their inability to grasp?

* * *

There are not digits enough to number the world's
          injustices. Or to fathom the quiet,
fierce power that eventually led Angulimala to mend his
          ways, quit fingering around.

For T., who Likens Me to a Rock

You say I am
a rock
sitting on the fringe,
soil-eyed, unmoved.

You are quite right,
a right little person
blindly flashing
a torch.
In fact,
I am one
with the darkness.

I swallow the moon
and stars,
blow the sun
a fatal kiss.

You, T., see
only what
that guiding sliver
of light
(or rather the night)
enable you
to see.

I have known
your big-toothed smile.
I draw the black
curtains
around me.

In the distance,
I hear
vampires chuckle.

Garlic, blood,
fish and loaves.

A pebble is picked
up and hurled
at a passing bat.

King

He takes off his head
at the end of the day
lays it aside
like a crown.

DOMINIC ALAPAT

When We Meet

in the streets
where hollow buildings
aflame ask
what do we do now
what do we say

outside the city
where land meets sea
birds are tearing the sky
to pieces
and all the alphabets
have fallen on the ground

lines lead to squares and circles
in the deep division
of the mad world here

round and round
the clusters of burning lights
flowing into the darkness.

In Search

of rhythm
the old poems tumble out
of the mind.

Like the black cupboard
in the green wall
I would climb

to sample the darkness
through the shelves
I would crawl

opening boxes
entranced by the silence
and lulled
by the softness there

lie back and dream
I guess I may have wanted
to be one of them

know what it was like
that sweet little red tin box
with the blue bird on its lid
quiet sitting in some cosy tree

in the sun
and the rows of medicines
with their intoxicating smell
taking me half a world away

until I begin to recognise
the bedsheets stacked till
the dark triangular roof

standing full of the softness
of welcome
telling me this is it
this is it
the real thing
the real universe
like a mother telling
her child
come
come home.

GJV PRASAD

Growing Old

In English he became someone's old man early
It took time in his Indian languages

But as he grew older and more respected not in English
English kept him young and with it

His wisdom he gained in years not in English
Alzheimer's stared at him in English

Soon he realised
He was growing old and unwanted
In English
And not in English

Road Kill

The streets rage in Delhi

They circle round your throat
Like pythons
In heat and cold
Rain and shine

Arterial and venal

A man killed a bus driver the other day
Another, a taxi driver, raped his customer
And then burnt her
A policeman simply picked up a brick
Not having been issued a revolver

Everyone is in a hurry
Everyone on a tight short leash
The red light always ready
To beat you before you begin

Stopping the poor
And daring to stop the rich

Someone has to get it

The streets rage in Delhi.

GOPIKRISHNAN KOTTOOR

The Mad Woman in the Shiva Temple

She is tantric with her young hands
Erect for a grief between her Shiva and her eyes.
For hours she has been standing
On one leg.
Her saffron robe dusts His third eye
In the shape of Agni.

She knows a man who seized her lips,
Who ripped open her breasts like a purse
Digging away its gold.

Now, what is love, Shiva, my Rudra?
Is it all about stealing the body?
Is it endlessly spearing the cleft
Between my growing moons
After that hangover
Between parted thighs?
You know it all, Rudra
Then why do you not speak?
Between you and me
There's nothing left to hide.
The one who took away all my gold
What did he gain?
What do we all gain, my Rudra
Except six feet underground?

The priest goes about his way
He doesn't even see her
As he fills Shiva with fresh *bael* leaves
Covering his third eye.

And Shiva sends her his gift
The small white snake upon his matted hair
Gliding upon the hollow of her cheek
Taking her six feet beneath,
Into New Moon darkness.

The Passport

The blue cloth hyacinths that father brought home from Bangkok
Stood heady on the carved round table in the black
                earthen vase.

Father said, 'Bangkok... is heaven'.
It was the only outside place he had been to.
Perhaps he had also been to the blind prostitutes
Pushing their pubic dark canoes into the night river
In Damnoen Saduak.
But if that, he did not tell mother.

Edge purpled, his kind of heaven,
The hyacinths blossomed in a dream of coloured fireworks,
Khlongs wet as lusty lips, and the great gold leaf Buddha
Lying like a fallen New York skyscraper.
Father had earned all that for himself, at last.

Every night he was at the carved round table
Dreaming of Bangkok.
Smoke-curls from his Player's cigarette chain
Roped the hyacinths in thick mist, till
They reeked entirely of tobacco dust.

Father adored his hyacinths. He watered them
With that longing look in his eyes, until
They closed into coma.

As he lay in the hospital, turning red-yellow,
The blue petals back home began to lose their shine,
Thirsting for the water of his eyes, his tobacco mouth.
They seemed quite prepared for what would be.

The day death encircled father in Easter mist,
Mother glued his best-looking photograph
Among the hyacinth petals, and laid his passport below,
In one last signature of love's quietening meridian.

It was as though, mother, she knew it all.

Of purple-edged hyacinths
Perpetual in father's watering eyes,
And of blank pages, sailing lost winds back home
To where the pubic dark canoes pushed upon night rivers
Of the blind girls in Damnoen Saduak.

JENNIFER ROBERTSON

To Kiss Like Caravaggio

is to feel a sudden shove: two
competing notions of
interference
and light: You and I, thieves
and Chiaroscuro love—love is nothing
but little delays
in succulence: an aftertaste
of blood swallowed
and spat out.
Only tongue remains. That
and a three-dimensional
culminating mouth
betrayed like Jesus.

Dimensions of a Swimming Pool for Narcissus

One can accept a Picasso woman with two noses, but an equivalent attempt in poetry baffles the same audience.
— *John Ashbery*

You wait in a world of headless lament,
inversely comparing audiences and people.
Who needs them? I say.
You make waivers for death and his fiancée,
measuring grief and loss in buckets,
creating Gods and his minions.
A pool for Cephissus' son?
Did you know he drowns, eventually? I say.
I stand alone, comparing oenophilia, and my addiction
to words. I count my children in reverse.
I remember hysterical midnight scuffles, infinite
sobs in between counting pages
Pessoa may or may not have written:
The Book of Disquiet, the weight of nothingness.
All poetry is bricolage, you say. You're not Ashbery
to carry the weight of your abstractions on your shoulder.
You're a nobody. You're not Emily.
What kind of a poet are you?
I am a rhinoceros but I'm also a nobody
I am convex, I say, curtaining the window.
My poems have two doors and no exit.
Every moment is almost two moments,
measured in calipers:
the width of the moment I hold on to
the breadth of the moment you let go

My poetry is the distance between these two moments:
millimetred.
However, the torque of my poetry
is beyond the jurisdiction of your tool box
because Narcissus swims in a different pool.

LINDA ASHOK

On His Second Marriage

when she married him
he was a tree with no branches
roots became stones
between him and my mother
his thick glasses
his bony vessel
with sparse body hair

then the berry trees. the ginger
and other herbs. they grew in abundance
in our portico
except

when he married her
she was no tree, no branches
an apparition
between her and my mother
his thick glasses
his rustic vessel
reminded her
of his sparse body hair

meantime,

my brother and I,
like protozoic timepieces
flourished on lime-washed walls.

Hard Water

You asked if we can stop the car midway and go for an ice-cream. Your eyes heavy with the speed of metal highway, your lips innocuous and patchy, you didn't have dreams for long nights...

I stared at you like a broken glass piece. I realised I was on the suicide seat holding fast to the moment, not willing to give up like a few Tibetan lanterns did that night.

I asked if you have been to see your mom lately. I wanted to ask about your family. I had asked several questions loud enough not to be heard but one, your favourite ice-cream flavour, if any.

Inside, it was getting warmer than before but I wanted our silence to be private. I drank my tongue and thought of spiders in ice farms.

I never wanted your hands to look into my face, never wanted your eyes to touch my hands. But I wanted both to sit me with trust and likening like the cold clouds hanging low on our car.

In that extreme moment, you wanted me to laugh in the voice of a caterpillar, bristle and break into a suave butterfly and forget measures in age and kind of fabric.

Life has never come in term with me and as usual, that night, ice-cream was only a scapegoat.

MALSAWMI JACOB

Zorami

Epitaph of
thousand dead
thousand living-dead
dreams dead

bard lamenting
turbid wars
ignoble deeds
lost treasures never found
souls lost in the search

wanderer in the night
seeking for a place to rest

shadow of *fiara tui*[1]

Waiting for another *thim zing*[2]?
The darkness at skull hill
covers all.

---

1   A Mizo mythical stream of the clearest, sweetest water
2   A time of total darkness in Mizo myth, when drastic transformations, such as a corpse becoming a constellation in the sky, took place

Note: Zorami is the name of a Mizo woman. She represents the fate of women in conflict situations in this poem.

MANI RAO

Postcard Aphrodite

1.
Ouranos leaned and pinched her nipples
Gaia forgot her sons lay in ambush
Even before he detached his thighs flanking the mountains
                                          her limbs arched for the meeting
Half swooning for his eyes leisurely grazing
It was not a memory   had never occurred
He was always so testy   (sons can be so crazy)
Recurrent dreams of a blade slicing his neck his blood
                                          seeding her body
When they sliced his testicles instead
His hands full on her breasts
Jerked a seizure
She ejaculated disbelief
Ouranos drained
Gaia sank

2.
Bright downward slash above
Ruddy Ocean below what
Remains of Sky

His pouches open paratroopers

Be anxious it's
Messy out there –
Wind reluctant
Waves nervous

Then laugh o how
Indifferent wave
Of average height &
No distinction
Lands the prize

3.
Recall that other time when the leaky punk Raktabija
                                               'bloodseed' battled Kali
The more she hacked the more he sprouted
Then Tongue stretched
Between Earth and Sky
Licked each drop
As it fell

4.
Fresh froth breaks
Bubbles on speed
Champagne-solemn

Water animates
Hands breasts waist
Crimped hair
Signature

Exactly when does she
Express her face
Translucent sea-squiggle
Aphrodite

Okeanos marks the moment
With a pause

Every wave rises
Reflects
Aphrodite gallery

5.
What is Aphrodite made of?

The impossible desire
Carried by Rivers
Buried in Ocean

You and I know it is memory   Gaia's
Aphrodite has none

Of one parent
Un-conflicted
She heads for America

6.
One hundred and fifty feet   stature
Shipwrecked hero
Face of commander

Beached on Ellis
Plankton-stained
Gulliver comes to mind

Little people probe her
Robe her
Hand her a torch
Hoist her on a pedestal
And crown her Statue Liberty

Poised since then
Open oyster shell

Desire ... Liberty

Fêted

1.
What does Odysseus do when
the Odyssey is done

Memory's man, house on fire
The story ate it all

Back from Iraq
Busy being a shape
A guard

Sleeps in the old bed
Dines the old way
Visitors none

The front hall scrubbed clean
All of Ithaca's young men
chatting in Hades

It's all about the oil they say
Finite fire

Odysseus, son of Laertes, father of Telemachus,
husband of constant Penelope, family man

A long night
One half in a dream, the other half
awake thinking about it

Over and over again, of Helen,
to the countrywomen

To the one-eyed scarecrow
in the fields said Nobody

2.
Another war-veteran Prometheus

Dented
De-fizzed
Rocket to space-junk
fell

Wayward washing
Ragged upon the crags

Flooded by the moon a startled thief
From the day he is engorged and cannot hide
Till the day he is mute and will not show

In the shadow of the eagle he sees keeping watch
A luscious rested tongue
And thirsts for it

3.
Bheeshma chooses when to die
After farewells, speeches and a drink

Last man standing, Yudhistira, has
a friend, a dog

The rest are soldiers, trees
Armor

Leaves
Star tips

End of day survivors
count spaces at the table

Face down at the bottom of that trench
Lots of hands and legs

4.
A child-minotaur branded monster
Thrown in a maze

Expect a labyrinth
A story

Alone uncastrated public object Minotaur
awaits a hero

We want a dizzying battle

Dodge! light-footed Theseus

Minotaur froths
Prisoner on d-day

5.
Arjuna retorts:

What do you know, Krishna,
what it is to be human?

Infant, on your knees
Excruciating waiting on teeth

From alphabet-soup to the world

Pregnant, determinate uterus
Milk in your breasts

Sleeping Dreaming

Two hands, two legs

Breath, bowels

Decrepit in the mirror

What do you know, Krishna

MANISHA LAKHE
Good Intentions

you again?
haven't i told you
i don't want to be
your good deed for the day?

of course i've been weeping.
the irrawady dolphins
have depleted, sad, no?
see, it says so on the newspaper
i've stuck on the windows.
oh that's for the sun.
he insists on intruding.
see that beam there? laserlike.
searching for proof
just like you.
so you can send me away.
i won't let you, you know.

sure, my friends are here
they've retreated in the shadows.
they know you won't try too hard.
you have to pick up Tina
from her dance lesson in twenty minutes.

don't look at me like that!
i haven't lost my mind you know
i've just let some friends in there.
i was so lonely after he left me.
yes, i did run after him

from the kitchen to the front door,
in my new stilettos,
i was chopping cabbage for coleslaw;
"don't leave me!" i cried,
but he was in a hurry, i suppose,
why wait when love has gone?
i think i must've tripped,
when i lunged for the door,
"don't leave me!" i said, he left
three and a half fingers
of his right hand,
i've kept them safe
right there, in the butter dish.

NABINA DAS

Poems from Rivers and Towns: Fireflies and Fish Conversations

those fireflies and rivers
wanted to get to the roads
over the banks of refugee shacks
over tumbling tempo hoods
over our embarrassed long and rounded vowels
just to smell the tar of dawki roads

and walk walk walk those monsoon-muddied paths
that brought us at the teetering end to ask:

will the fish wake up and recognize us?

***

the valley people spoke of a beautiful fish-woman
who came up to the river shore on full moon nights to taste salt
of the sands, of the tongues of pahar line cooing through tunnels
where trains ran headlong with faces hidden

they spoke of a black horse on dawn's back
a horse that munched on rising sunrays
the pasture of light
and showed them the way beyond where the magur
                      had swum away

did you say the woman was a mermaid?
in fact, she was all fish
a woman who could swim through doors like some of us

***

once through the milling crowd we had burrowed in
small change in tiny hand and counting trees of legs
we were small
we wouldn't answer strangers and princes and clowns
even though the fair with its Ferris Wheels had encircled us
and the crowd became the rising sea
surging in us the fear of the known
hearing hey mister acharjee babu and oh missus prerona debi

no we aren't running away from home

once through with the milling crowd we stopped
at this lane by the strange
house that was lonely
we got home with the fair in our head
circling like afternoon pigeons while
someone screamed from afar

    – come see the little girl cut in halves
    come, come see her live and speak!

***

my uncle stuffed fireflies in his pocket
to go to the barak's banks
fireflies as baits for the fish he secretly listened to
he wooed the fish and told them stories
i'm told on gibbous nights they too
came up to tell him tales
truths and half lies
of bodies pushed under

of sad brides sleeping under waves
of fingers and rings carved on bed-mud
of money stash swaying like algae
of keys to homes that stood on one legs before falling asunder
of map etchings thrown to the fish's mouths
of words turned into sludge
of gods who wouldn't be worshipped in households

the fishing rods stretched their length
drooped in one corner of my uncle's house
they carried the load of those stories
until fireflies returned to listen to them
glittering in dark corners like children's eyes

i've seen them hum together
before the railway line outside went home
and conversations were served in coffee cups

ROCHELLE POTKAR

Transmogrified

He was first a snake and was in love with her – a she-snake. And then he moulted, and after he moulted, he was a turtle, and he met another she-turtle and fell in love with her. When he de-shelled after years, he became a four-legged animal, black spots sprouting over his fur, and he fell for a leopard. He moved this way through the jungles, the savannas, the deserts, the skies, through the oceans, the air, the land and beneath it, changing and changing and meeting and falling in love with new she-species.

The lovers he left behind did not change. They were who they were. The same.

They were individualistic so to speak, but now they were also heart-broken and full of hate for him – the one who had left in the middle of, sometimes, passionate love-making.

They had no idea how it was to live so many lives in one life like him.

To take no breaks with rebirths from being mosquito to man.

Sometimes evolution and progress is so fast, blessings and curses are all mixed up, and One.

Raw Forms

From the first smells of wet mud
to this heartache
you were the perfect shaft of sun
that passed through my stained-glass window
so I could watch the carcass
of a fallen rainbow.

It is not you alone that caused this misfortune.

It takes two distinct kinds
to mix and merge
to produce something different.

People with uncommon atomic arrangements…
like tin and copper,
nickel and palladium,
copper and zinc,
to crystallize into
bronze, white gold, brass…

Take aluminium, for example.
They say it is soft, malleable
but with another softie: copper
it becomes hard, strong: aluminium alloy.

take acetylene that blends with oxygen
to become the hottest burning fuel.

Take chocolate with its vanilla and cocoa gradients,
Or milk in its tea variants,
rain running on diverse mud, land, soil.

You get the drift?

I don't want you to change.
I don't want me to change.
But there are gaps in our atomic lattice
                          – sieves large enough
through which I fall and bruise.

Most things in its raw forms are not stable:
diamond, platinum, potassium,
gold, sugar,
or love.

I have tried leaving.
I really have.
But like a soul not allowed to leave
its battered accident body
I am a molecule pulled back.

Our story is not over.

So stay with me till we are
heated by ennui,
melted by its reasons,
hardened by the seasons,
softened by its perceptions.

One day our lattices shall carry
our faith, our patience,
our knowing of each other
stronger than our arms could ever hold.

We will weld and meld,
to form the perfect-imperfect
stable substance.

SARABJEET GARCHA

The Gurdwara with a Bell

It took me a kneel-down
to know that a garlanded photo frame
can give more joy than
the god tucked within,

that the damp grey dregs
of burnt incense
are laden with a coy
catechism of slow fire,

that a deity can easily
be coaxed into submission
or roped in by the silence
slithering in prayer
and half-whispers clung to
the throat's drumskin tautness.

It took me supine surrender
to see that a copper bell
fastened to a roof beam can
resonate reveries much before
finger touches clapper
or eyelid kisses sclera,

that the body rejoices
in the quiet which swirls
in the closed-room dusk of

heat-swollen afternoons, when
the primal yearning of flesh
makes the bones quiver

with the fear of vehement
sinning in the very midst
of saints, ever watchful
in their still-life serenity.

Mountain Maker

Did the mountain maker
build the thing up
stone by unhewn stone
from foot to crest

and leave the rocks astray
to heal the hollows of their
supple cavities
with mud marinated
by the turning of seasons?

Or did he knead
a lump of loose brown soil
on flatland
like jaggery gone viscous
in a summer without end

and mould it with the lined
shell of bone and flesh,
his fingers slapping the sides
like barn slats,
his palm sheltering the top
like a shrine's cupola

to check
with a potter's precision
the scattering
of the only knickknacks
rescued from a lifetime of
teasing a little melody
out of the plastic chaos
of claycraft?

And then maybe he sprinkled
a neat net of crevices on
the first such malleable mound
to make the underlying mortar
immortal with green crepe,

an unmistakable bookmark
to his favourite passages
on the spherical tome he
keeps dipping into,
never tires of.

SHIKHA MALAVIYA

Hiraeth

After Nirbhaya

You are the one with more than one name: Braveheart, Lightning, Fearless One. A star is a star is a star is a star. Is what you are. Aspiring astronomer's dream, galactic dirge, lover's requiem.

Celestial layers crumble at the touch, scattering savory stardust. Traveling at the speed of light, you halt in front of a hammock made of stars. Soul pinballing through the universe, zig zag zoom, Mars to Jupiter to Neptune, you break off a corner from Saturn's rings. Too salty you think, as it falls through your tongue. Touch is taste and taste is touch. 5-4-3-2-1. The black hole unfurls its movie screen to show big and little bangs. Today, the movie is you. The body you carefully maintained, oiled, plucked, rubbed, anointed, scrubbed—undone by a thread's pull, the silver one binding you to earth, broken by betel nutstained canines. They bite into you tasting type-A blood and like plaster of Paris the skin holds impressions, soaked with local hooch and seasonal employment. The breast with *Kannagi's* scent is lobbed at their faces, and your uterus, an umbrella, opens out to shield the rain. Albatross. You feel its ancient weight between breasts and legs. *Nose cut off, turned to stone, following him into the fire,* because that was always your designated place. A city's neck grows heavier, as you writhe on an empty road, intestines uncoiled like Rapunzel's hair, willing someone to grab hold. Intubated, medicated, operated on—once they find you, they outsource you, each

breath more precious than gold. *'Braveheart! Lightning! Fearless One!'* News anchors, politicians, protestors chant. The hospital clock ticks like a metronome, inhale exhale, inhale exhale. And as they name and blame and pray, you slip out quietly from the day. Stardust now, getting used to deep space, you zig, zag and zoom from place to place. A star is a star is a star is a star. Is what you are. An albatross in the Milky Way, soaring in a figure eight, that some would
call infinity.

Nirbhaya (Fearless one in Hindi) was the name given to a young physiotherapist who was beaten and gang-raped in New Delhi, India, in December 2012, after boarding a bus. She succumbed to her injuries and died thirteen days after the incident, creating furore and outrage across the nation.

Kannagi- The central character of the Tamil epic Silapathikaram (100-300 CE), who took revenge on the King of Madurai, for wrongly imposing the death penalty on her husband Kovalan, by lobbing off her breast in anger, while cursing the city, inciting its destruction.

Hiraeth *A Welsh word that literally translates as 'longing', homesickness for a home to which you cannot return, a home that never was. Homesickness tinged with grief or sadness over the lost or departed.*

Genocide Gatehouse
After RB Kitaj's painting 'If Not, Not'

A madman's
paradise
its slogan
welded
to the entrance gates
Arbeit Macht Frei
fringed by
charred palms
swaying under
umber skies

I stole Matisse's
paintbrush
while he was
sleeping
siphoning off
colors
from
other lives
a dead man
with his boot
removed
a breathing one
on his belly
staring
at our love
as you sit
naked
beside me
a star burned

into your skin

You ask me
to trace it
with my tongue
taste the light
that always follows
darkness
and when I do
my mouth fills up
with ashes
the color
of azaleas

SRIDALA SWAMI

Daybreak

It is not so much the blade of day
that slices the morning's eye open
as that it begins anyway
uncoerced and softly-spoken

breathing in the yeasty
rising breeze;   and warms its fingers
on the rose-glow of clouds steep-
stacked and neat-racked by the sun's balusters;

begins despite the clamour and the war cry
of the blown conch, the dawn prayer
the challenge of javelin voices that vie
to fling their chants through the air.

Morning comes like a man used to
lying awake waiting for tomorrow.

Red Chillies

113° Fahrenheit on
the third day of May.
In Guntur
every red chilli in the market
as if by concert
bursts
into sharp-tongued flames

and

the air breaks
into loud
applause.

No Thirteen Ways About It

The beauty of inflections
Or the beauty of innuendoes
                    - Wallace Stevens

Slant your rhymes which way you will
Varuna, each wave only sways to one will

Plant your deep-rooted feet upon the shore
Abandon for a while the shifting clay of your will

Show me a face I know as little as I know mine
I'll follow my fingers and obey the dictates of their will

Though the scrapyards are filled with abandoned words
We could salvage a few from decay if you will

Songs the birds whirled in the autumn winds
Dance still unruly swayed by no one will

Long only for the elusive and contrary, Sridala
Spike the everyday upon the point of your will

UMA NARAYAN

Terminus

Victoria Terminus. Named after a Queen whose Raj
has long since ended, it has since been re-baptized
to honor a more local royal line who gnawed at the
 thick haunches of Empire from the forts and battlements
 whose ruins stud the mountains of the state. In any case,
neither history has really managed to secure purchase
on the name. VT, we all call it, just the initials unmoored from
the name, VT from where long-distance trains spoke out
to traverse the distances of our sub-continent.

I am not sure why it was the fashion for facades
of colonial railway stations to mimic the lineaments
of Gothic cathedrals. It stands amid the welter of Bombay
traffic, its expanse of weighty stone and soaring buttresses
proclaiming its monumental, sacramental status within
the geography of urban sprawl. Its thin spires reach tentatively
upwards to touch the pregnant swell of gray monsoon sky.

Even the interior conveys a sense of church; the ornamental
grill of the ticket window suggests a concealed cassock rather
than a harried clerk selling tickets, provokes an impulse
to confession. Forgive me, Father, for I have sinned.
                        Shrive me,
absolve me. as you sell me my ticket to Poona. The pale light

filters through the stained-glass windows, an occasional beam
floats across the high dark expanse to touch a
                        transfigured passenger

like the Holy Ghost. Even the noisiness and clamor seem
to flatten out
to hum, the sound of a invisible choir chanting at a distance.

Something about the hunched, patient posture of those
waiting for long-distance trains reminds me of prayer. You can
almost hear the whispered words rising like incense, wafting
to the high dark ceiling, reaching out for intercession. Please
let the train arrive in time, please get me out of here. Please,
please, let the train be late, postpone the hour of my departure.
Please let her reach her destination safely. Please let him return
again. Return to me. Return soon. You can almost smell
                              the sorrow
of impending distance, the scent of anticipated loss, hear the
silent liturgies of aching, breaking hearts.

Eyes gaze dully at the metal of the empty tracks, where
A train will too soon pull in, too soon pull out, carrying
Away those who matter, into the distance that stretches
beyond the limits of eye's reach, into that vanishing point
where parallel lines meet.

USHA AKELLA

Bridges of Struga
(Ghazal)

The dark glass of night shatters. Will the Call to Prayer
        listen to poetry tonight?
The river's wine flows, there are homeless poets fragile on
        the bridge tonight.

From a pen slips a river, people's shadows in the water are
        stone-like and grave high,
Night's tresses knot, a poet spreads out his cloak on the
        banks by a bridge in the night.

There are bridges of words and words metastasize,
        metastasize like monuments,
On the banks are churches, in reflections mosques are seen
        from the bridge tonight.

Pale stain of veins of saints in battered brickwork,
        mountains rise like serrated hearts,
Two dark breasts rise from the earth, in the cavity within,
        Jesus is dining in Mecca tonight.

Who is selling and who is buying in the bazar, one sells
        his heart, one his desire,
Who is going, who is coming; ride winged steeds of
        poems to reach Jerusalem tonight.

Hushed air; the poet passes through a monk's cell small as
        an eye; poetry is silenced,

The bridge is land's yearning for the river, everything
swells high on the bridge tonight.

All is plausible on the scroll of the bridge, a city rewrites
her story, Alexander rides high,
Poetry is humble on the square, poets knows the ghazal is
never finished on the bridge tonight.

Struga poetry evenings: Oldest poetry festival in the world renowned for the 'Bridges' event that takes place on a bridge on the river Drim. Poets from around the world assemble to read from a podium, a river running under. It is said that 10,000 people gather to hear the poets.
words metastasize: The new nationalist Macedonia on display rift with monuments reflecting strident nationalist pride.

Two dark breasts: Black old mosque converted to the Macedonian museum of art in Skopje. There's a painting of Jesus in a prayer niche facing Mecca.

Kalishta monastery: Has a tiny cell of a monk with a narrow doorway

Jerusalem

Jerusalem shall I dare say your tales
with this foreign tongue
as I spin like a top in your streets?
Shall I enter your gates as you lie
under the fingertips of a golden menorah,
what badge shall I show your armed men keeping peace,
When I listen to a mother calling for her children
in fields of invisible ears and tongueless tongues,
and old walls tremble with secrets, flags and burdens
and Time, the deathless watchman, prowls your streets,
when the mint in your tea refreshes my tongue,
and bread fills my stomach and I walk, walk
the walk of Via Dolorosa on the palm of the city
pointing different directions
with more than one minotaur at its center,
When I climb Mt. Olives and see dead men waiting
like chocolates in boxes to be opened,
when I see the patience and the impatience of waiting,
and prophets' names, too many to remember
cast shadows on your streets, shall I ask for permission,
to enter, shall I dare stand by a wall, join lines
of people in eternal mourning, yearning, shall I join
my grief to theirs and ask for temples to be built,
idol of idols, how shall I gain entry?
You, the navel of this earth, where people rooted
to salt, faith, loyalty, three times over,
like three rivers flowing separately,
between your messianic apocalyptic banks,
What message can I bring as balm for your wounds?
All messages are known to you, they are coded
in your stones in the cursive of prophets,

city of walls, stones, earth, restoration, air,
light, sky, blood, hope, tears, wail, lament,
city of streets wagging many languages,
where past present future coexist as solemn triplets,
Shall I dare change the cartography of religion,
stand under the golden dome and let fly
a new litany longing to be rewritten.

The Rosary of Latitudes

If I told you, I have been shown cities
like a procession of bejeweled elephants
of ponderous gait,
and the earth took their load,

And the latitudes passed under my feet like
skipping ropes under a young girl's quick step,

If I told you, in one city,
I sat on the steps of a great plaza,
and watched humanity as if for the very last time,
and knew it was the very last time,
and this time around,
it is time to say goodbye,

In many cities I stood in long lines
for Darshan, my devotion
was the eye that looked
at the stone for awakening,
I make this confession...

I was taken on a ferry ride to see tiny islands afloat
on water like spilled mustard seeds, if I told you,
on one such island...
I knew I was more alone than any of them,

In another, where a river is a silent vein in the skin
of a lake, a poet tried hard to light the unlit wicks of my eyes,
they only gave out the smoke of incense at funeral rites,

In one town, high in a mountain plastered with porcelain plates,
Such places exist! In such a town, where anything could happen,
I walked with a poet and we walked as two sides of a
                      ravine with
no connecting bridge,

In one city, I thought I lost love,
the streets of that city became the lines of a Ghazal
mourning repeatedly, in that city again, I learnt I lost nothing,
I found myself at the borders of that city when I left it,

In one city, I saw monuments of loveliness
rise from my imagination
and hover in the twilight like rose-tinted pearls,
I walked through the pages of the Arabian nights,
The things I saw in that land,
filled my pockets with dreams to hand out,
yet this city was not a magic lamp to rub and
wish for the beloved
it merely twirled in its dervish robes
lost on its own axis,

In one city, I walked hoping to see him somewhere,
And then I looked in another city,
And another, and another, I returned empty-handed,
There were cities that would not meet my gaze,
Not one of them told me to stop looking,
Not one of them says it yearns for me,

If I told you of the lovers I have seen,
And the lovers searching,
And the lovers thinking they have found,

And the lovers making by,
And the lovers deluded,
And the lovers sullen and silent,
And the lovers like
the soundless strings of violins,
in these cities… and I safe in the fortress of my skin,
If I tell you I have been sinless and heavy-hearted for it,

If I told you, all the latitudes
are the unread lines of my love letter…

The Contributors
2013

ABHA IYENGAR is a British Council-certified creative writing mentor and an award-winning poet, author, editor and translator. Abha has been a writer-in-residence at the *Sangam House Residency* and received the *Lavanya Sankaran Writing Fellowship* for 2009-2010. Her short fiction, *The Marshlands*, was shortlisted in the DNA-Out of Print short story contest (2015). Abha's story, *The High Stool*, was nominated for the Million Writers Award. Her poem-film, *Parwaaz* (flight) won the Special Jury Prize at Patras, Greece. Her works include *Yearnings, Flash Bites, Many Fish to Fry, The Gourd Seller & Other Stories, The Tattoo at her Throat, The Orange Straw Murders* and *The Full Platter*. She has co-edited an anthology titled *The Other*, and curated and edited two flash fiction anthologies titled *Kintsugi* and *Skin*.

ADIL JUSSAWALLA (*born 1940*) is among the key founders of a new mid-20th century Indian modernist poetry in English, according to *Frontline Magazine* (February 8, 2024). He edited the influential anthology *New Writing in India*, (Penguin, 1974) and was editor of the publishing house XAL-Praxis. Author of collections such as *Land's End, Missing Person, Earth (Poems for Veronik), Trying to Say Goodbye, Shorelines, The Right Kind of Dog* and *The Magic Hand of Chance*, among others, Jussawalla received the Sahitya Akademi award in 2014 and Tata Literature Live! Poet Laureate Award in 2021. The poems reproduced here with his permission are from *Land's End* and *Trying to Say Goodbye*.

ANAMIKA Prof. Anamika teaches literature in English at Satyawati College (University of Delhi). Her doctoral thesis is on the reception of John Donne across the ages. She has published extensively also in the areas of Translating Studies and Gender Justice. Besides eight volumes of criticism, she has published seven well-received novels in Hindi. Three of her novels, *Dus Dware ka Peenjara, Aienasaz* and *Trin Dhari Oat* have won national awards and been staged as major stage productions. In 2020, she received the Sahitya Akademi Award for her poetry collection *Tokri Mein Digant*. Poems from her other poetry collections, such as *Anushtup, Khurduri Hatheliyan, Doob - Dhan, Pani Ko Sab Yaad Tha* and *Band Raston Ka Safar* are prescribed at different Universities and have been rendered into languages such as Malayalam, Marathi, Bangla, Punjabi, Oriya, Kannada, Korean, Russian and English. She herself is an avid translator and is also the founder-editor of a bilingual journal called *Pashyantee*.

Dr. Anamika's essays on womanist discourse in Hindi too have been translated into many languages and she has translated the works of Rilke, Neruda, Doris Lessing, Octavio Paz, and fellow women poets extensively. Her major English publications include *Transplanting British Poetry in Indian Classrooms, Donne Criticism Down the Ages, Post-War Women Poets: Treatment of Love and Death, Feminist Poetics: Where Kingfishers Catch Fire, Translating Racial Memory, Weaving a Nation: Proto-Feminist Writing in Hindi and Urdu*.

ANAND THAKORE is a poet and Hindustani classical vocalist. Thakore spent a part of his childhood in Britain and has lived in India since then. *In Praise of Bone, Seven Deaths and Four Scrolls, Mughal Sequence, Elephant Bathing, Selected Poems* and *Waking in December* are his six published collections of verse. He is the founder of Harbour Line, a Mumbai-based publishing collective, and of Kshitij, a group devoted to the creation of interactive performance spaces for musicians. In 2024, the Drunken Boat Global Classics series featured his work in *Three Indian Poets: Arundhathi Subramaniam, Deepankar Khiwani and Anand Thakore.*

ANJU MAKHIJA is an award-winning poet, playwright and translator. She has published three poetry collections: *View from the Web, Pickling Season* and *Poems Grow With You*; co-translated *Freedom & Fissures* and *Seeking the Beloved* – the mystical verse of Shah Abdul Latif; co-edited three anthologies related to women, Indo-English theatre and young readers. She is also the author of *Mumbai Traps: Collected Plays. Changing, Unchanging: New & Selected Poems* is forthcoming. Anju's awards include the Sahitya Akademi English Translation Prize, The All-India Poetry Competition, the BBC World Regional Poetry Prize and The Charles Wallace Trust Scholarship. She was on the English Advisory Board of the Sahitya Akademi, New Delhi, for five years and has co-founded the Pondicherry/Auroville Poetry Festival.

ANNIE ZAIDI writes poetry, non-fiction, fiction, and scripts for stage and screen. She is the author of *'Love Stories # 1 to 14'*, and the co-author of *'The Bad Boy's Guide to the Good Indian Girl'*. Her first collection of essays, *'Known Turf: Bantering with Bandits and Other True Tales'*, was shortlisted for the Crossword (non-fiction) book prize and was translated into Italian as *'I Miei Luoghi'*. She writes poetry and plays in both English and Hindi. *'Jaal'* and *'So Many Socks'* were performed in Mumbai in 2012. Her work has appeared in anthologies like *Mumbai Noir; Women Changing India; Journeys Through Rajasthan; 21 Under 40; India Shining, India Changing;* and in journals like *The Little Magazine, Pratilipi, Out of Print; Caravan and Desilit.* Her novel, *Prelude To A Riot,* won the Tata Literature Live! Awards for Book of the Year 2020. In 2019, she won The Nine Dots Prize for her work *Bread, Cement, Cactus* and in 2018 she won The Hindu Playwright Award for her play, *Untitled-1.* Annie's other works include *Crush,* (poetry), *The Good Indian Girl* (short stories), and *Gulab* (a novella).

ANUPAMA RAJU is a poet, literary journalist, communications professional and translator. She has published two poetry collections, *Bitter Gourd* and *Nine,* and a novel, *C.* Anupama has been translating short fiction and poetry from Malayalam into English. As a freelance contributor and columnist, she writes for *The Hindu* and *Scroll.in.* A Charles Wallace Fellow at the University of Kent, Canterbury, Anupama was also Writer-in-Residence at Le Centre Intermondes, La Rochelle. She is an alumna of Women's Christian College, Stella Maris College and Madras Christian College, Chennai. She lives in India and works for a US-based technology services company.

ARUNDHATHI SUBRAMANIAM is the award-winning author of fourteen books of poetry and prose, including the recent poetry volume, *Love Without a Story,* and a book of essays on contemporary women on sacred journeys, *Women Who Wear Only Themselves.* Her other work includes two acclaimed sacred poetry anthologies, *Wild Women* and *Eating God* and the bestselling biography of a mystic, *Sadhguru: More Than a Life.* She has received the Sahitya Akademi Award for Poetry (2020), the Mahakavi Kanhaiyalal Sethia Poetry Award, the Raza Award for Poetry (2009), the inaugural Khushwant Singh Poetry Prize, the Charles Wallace Fellowship (for a three-month writing residency at the University of Stirling) in 2003; the Visiting Arts Fellowship for a poetry tour of the UK (organized by the Poetry Society) in 2006; and the Homi Bhabha Fellowship in 2012. A long-standing arts critic, anthologist, performing arts curator and poetry editor, she divides her time between Mumbai, Chennai and New York.

ARVIND KRISHNA MEHROTRA's recent books are *Book of Rahim & Other Poems* (Literary Activism/ Westland India and Shearsman Books UK) and a translation of Vinod Kumar Shukla's poems *Treasurer of Piggy Banks* (Literary Activism/Westland India and Circumference Books US). His first full-length collection of poems, *Nine Enclosures*, was published by Clearing House in 1976.

EUNICE de SOUZA *(1940-2017)* taught at St Xavier's College in Mumbai for over thirty years and retired as Head of Department. Her first collection of poems, *Fix*, appeared in 1979 and was followed by *Women in Dutch Painting.* (1988), *Ways of Belonging* (1990) and *Selected and New Poems.* (1994). She has written two novels, *Dangerlok* (Penguin, 2001) and *Dev & Simran: A Novel.* (Penguin, 2003). Her collection of interviews *Conversations with Indian Poets* was published by OUP in 2001. She also edited *Nine Indian Women Poets: An Anthology.* (OUP, 2001), *101 Folktales From India* (2004), *Purdah: An Anthology.* (OUP, 2004), *Women's Voices: Selections from Nineteenth and Early Twentieth Century Indian Writing in English.* (OUP, 2004), *Early Indian Poetry in English: An Anthology 1829-1947.* (OUP, 2005), *The Satthianadhan Family Album.* (Sahitya Akademi, 2005), with Melanie Silgardo, *These My Words: The Penguin Book of Indian Poetry (2012).* The poems reproduced here, with the poet's permission, are from *A Necklace of Skulls: Collected Poems* (Penguin Books India, 2009).

GAYATRI MAJUMDAR is editor, publisher and founder of critically acclaimed Indian literary journal, *The Brown Critique* (since 1995). Gayatri began her career as a journalist for the Press Trust of India and *The Independent* (India) in Mumbai. Her books include *A Song for Bela* (a novel), four poetry collections *Shout* (Sampark, 2000), *I Know You Are Here* and *A Warm Place with No Memory* (Red River, 2019 and 2023), *The Dream Pod* (Copper Coin; 2022), non-fiction *The lotus of the heart* and *Home* Anthology (co-Ed.) Gayatri is co-founder of Pondicherry Poets and curates the annual Pondicherry/Auroville Poetry Festival. She also features poets and musicians on The Brown Critique, Gayatri Majumdar's YouTube channel. Gayatri lives by the sea in Pondicherry, India.

GIEVE PATEL *(1940-2023),* an influential figure in Indian English poetry, was a writer and painter, with three books of poems – *Poems* (pub. Nissim Ezekiel, Bombay, 1966), *How Do You Withstand, Body* (Clearing House, Bombay, 1976) and *Mirrored, Mirroring* (Oxford University Press, Madras, 1991). He conducted an annual poetry workshop for school students at Rishi Valley School in Andhra Pradesh for more than two decades. *Poetry with Young People* (Sahitya Akademi, New Delhi, 2007) is an anthology of poems written by these students. He also wrote three plays, all of which have been performed. A collection, *Mister Behram and Other Plays*, was published by Seagull Books, Calcutta, in 2007, and his *Collected Poems*, published by Poetrywala, appeared in 2017. His poems have been included in anthologies in India and in other countries. He is considered to be one of India's most important painters, of the generation that first came to public notice in the seventies. A doctor by profession, he worked as a medical practitioner in urban and rural India.

HARISH NAMBIAR is the author of *Defragmenting India: Riding A Bullet Through The Gathering Storm*. He has also written the Culture Counter column in The *Economic Times*. His poems have been included in the *British Council anthology of Indian Poetry* and won an honourable mention in the inter-board poetry competition.

HEMANT DIVATE is a celebrated Marathi poet, editor, publisher, translator and poetry activist. He is the author of eight poetry collections in Marathi. His most recent book in Marathi is *Paranoia*, which was awarded the Govt. of Maharashtra's Kavi Keshavsut Award. Divate's poems have been translated into more than 30 international languages. In translation, he has a book in Spanish, Irish, Arabic, German, Estonian and Kannada, apart from four in English. His poems figure in numerous Marathi, English, Spanish and Slovenian anthologies. Divate is the founder-editor of the Marathi little magazine *AbhidhaNantar*, credited for providing a platform to new poets and for enriching the post-nineties Marathi literary scene. Divate is credited with changing the Marathi literary scene through *AbhidhaNantar* and the Indian English poetry scene through his imprint Poetrywala. He has participated in numerous international poetry and literature festivals. His publishing house, Paperwall Publishing has published (under its imprint Poetrywala) more than 150 poetry collections. Hemant is the founder and director of the Mumbai Poetry Festival.

HOSHANG MERCHANT is the author of more than 20 books of poetry, and four critical studies. He edited India's first gay anthology *Yaraana: Gay Writing from India*. His works include *Secret Writings of Hoshang Merchant, Bellagio Blues, Forbidden Sex/Texts, Indian Homosexuality, The Man Who Would Be Queen: Autobiographical Fiction* and *Sufiana: Poems*. Born in Mumbai in 1947, Merchant has a Masters from Occidental College, Los Angeles, and studied Renaissance and Modernism at Purdue. He is an Indian poet deeply rooted in his family traditions while at the same time expressing the glory and pain of being a pioneering poet in gay India.

JEET THAYIL is the author of five novels and five poetry collections, including *These Errors Are Correct*, which won the 2012 Sahitya Akademi Award. He is the editor of *The Penguin Book of Indian Poets* (2022). His novel *Narcopolis* was shortlisted for the 2012 Man Booker Prize and won the 2013 DSC Prize for South Asian Literature. Thayil is also the author of *The Book of Chocolate Saints*, a novel and cultural history of Bombay's poets. The poems reproduced here, with the author's permission, are from *These Errors are Correct*, published by Tranquebar in 2008 and Penguin Random House in 2022.

JERRY PINTO has two collections of poetry to his credit: *Asylum and Other Poems* and *I Want a Poem and Other Poems*. His book of poems for children *Tickle Me, Don't*

Tickle Me and Other Poems for Magnificent, Turbo-Loaded, Triple-Charged Children is now used in Indian schools. With Neela Bhagwat, he has translated the hymns of the women saints of Maharashtra in *The Ant Who Swallowed the Sun: the Abhangs of Marathi Women Saints*. Shanta Gokhale and he have worked together to produce parallel translations of the poet-saint Tukaram in *Behold! The Word is God*. He has also translated the poems of Narayan Surve as *In That Mill I Too Was Forged*. His novel *Em and the Big Hoom* won the Windham-Campbell Prize from Yale and the Sahitya Akademi award from India's Academy of Letters. In other lives he has been active in the sphere of child rights and the library movement. He is waiting for his next poem.

K SRILATA is a poet, fiction writer, translator and academic based in Chennai. She received the first prize in the All India Poetry Competition organised by the British Council and The Poetry Society (India). She was also awarded the Unisun British Council Poetry Award and the Charles Wallace writing residency at University of Stirling. Her works include *Seablue Child, Arriving Shortly, Writing Octopus, Bookmarking the Oasis, The Unmistakeable Presence of Absent Humans* and *Three Women in a Single-Room House*. Srilata has also translated from Tamil to English two millennia worth of poetry titled *Rapids of a Great River: The Penguin Book of Tamil Poetry* along with Lakshmi Holmstrom and Subashree Krishnaswamy.

K SATCHIDANANDAN *(born May 28 1946)* is a poet, playwright, fiction writer, travel writer, editor and social and literary critic in Malayalam/English. With more than 70 original works and 30 books of translations of poetry from across the world, Satchidanandan has won several awards including the Sahitya Akademi Award, The Poet Laureate Award from Tata Litfest, Knighthood from the Government of Italy, India-Poland Friendship Medal and Dante Medal from Ravenna. Recent works in English include *While I Write* (Selected Poems, Harper Collins) *The Misplaced* Objects and Other Poems (Sahitya Akademi, Delhi), *The Missing Rib* (Collected Poems 1973-2015), *Not Only the Oceans* and *Singing in the Dark: A Global Anthology of Poetry Under LockDown*, both edited, pub. Penguin-Random House). Satchidanandan is considered a pioneer of modern Malayalam poetry.

KEKI N. DARUWALLA *(born 1937)* is a major Indian poet and short story writer with over 12 collections. His first book of poems, *Under Orion* from Writers Workshop, appeared in 1970, and his *Collected Poems* (1970 – 2005) was published by Penguin Books. His first novel, *For Pepper and Christ*, came out in 2009. Daruwalla received the Sahitya Akademi Award in 1984 for his poetry collection, *The Keeper of the Dead* and the Commonwealth Poetry Prize for Asia in 1987 for his book *Landscapes*. He was awarded the Padma Shri in 2014. He has also received the Poet Laureate award at the Tata Literature Live! Mumbai Litfest, 2017. Daruwalla is a former IPS officer. He served as Special Secretary, Research and Analysis Wing (RAW) and retired as Chairman, Joint Intelligence Committee.

LAKSMISREE BANERJEE is an award-winning poet / author, literary critic, educationist, editor and practising radio & TV vocalist. She is an International Senior Fulbright Scholar, Commonwealth Scholar and National Scholar from Calcutta University, a UGC Post-Doctoral Research Awardee and Former Vice Chancellor & Pro Vice Chancellor of Kolhan University, Eastern India. She has eleven books of poetry (with two more forthcoming) and several academic publications, including books. She is the recipient of two international awards for Lifetime Achievement in Art & Literature and has also received the International Panorama Award for Poetry, Kala Ratnam Award, Asian Literary Society Women Achievers' Award, Connoisseur of Literary Arts of Asia & Tunisia Award, Literoma Laureate Award for Lifetime Achievement, Sahitya Akademi's Avishkar Award as "a Scholar-Artiste & Poet Musician", among others.

MALAY ROYCHOUDHURY *(1939 - 2023)* was a Bengali poet, best known for launching the Hungryalist movement in the 1960s. The author of more than seventy books, including novels, poetry collections, drama, short stories, essays, he also translated Blake, Ginsberg, Tzara, Cocteau, Cendrars, Lorca, Mayakovsky, Rimbaud, Rajkamal Chaudhary and many others. He edited the literary periodical ZEBRA and co-edited anthologies of Postmodern Bangla Poetry and Postmodern Bangla Short Stories which include writers from both India and Bangladesh. He was prosecuted for his poem *Stark Electric Jesus* in 1964-66. He refused to accept a Sahitya Akademi award, the Government of India's highest award for literature.

MANOHAR SHETTY has published several books, including *A Guarded Space, Borrowed Time, Domestic Creatures: Poems, Body Language, Creatures Great and Small, Personal Effects* and *Morning Light*. Shetty has been a Homi Bhabha and Senior Sahitya Akademi Fellow. He was awarded a Fellowship by Fundacao Oriente. He edited *Goa Today*, a monthly magazine, for eight years. He is also the editor of *Ferry Crossing: Short Stories from Goa* (Penguin India), which has gone into multiple editions and became a standard text in colleges around Goa. Shetty has also edited a special edition on English language poets of India for *Poetry Wales*.

MEENA KANDASAMY described by the *Independent* as a 'one-woman, agit-prop literary-political movement', is a poet, writer, translator, anti-caste activist and academic. Her corpus includes two poetry collections, *Touch* (2006) and *Ms Militancy* (2010), as well as three novels, *The Gypsy Goddess* (2014), the Women's Prize short-listed *When I Hit You* (2017) and *Exquisite Cadavers* (2019). In 2022, she was elected as a Fellow of the Royal Society of Literature (FRSL) and was also awarded the PEN Hermann Kesten Prize for her writing and work as a 'fearless fighter for democracy, human rights and the free word.' Her latest published work is *Tomorrow Someone Will Arrest You*, a collection of political poetry of the last decade.

MUSTANSIR DALVI is a poet, translator and editor. He has three books of poems — *Brouhahas of Cocks* (Poetrywala, 2013), *Cosmopolitician* (Poetrywala, 2018) and *WALK* (Yavanika Press, 2020/Poetrywala, 2021). He is widely anthologised, and his poems have been translated into French, Croatian, Gujarati, Marathi and Hindi. Mustansir Dalvi's 2012 English translation of Muhammad Iqbal's influential *Shikwa* and *Jawaab-e-Shikwa* from the Urdu as *Taking Issue and Allah's Answer* (India Penguin Modern Classics) has been described as 'insolent and heretical' and makes Iqbal's verse accessible to the modern reader. *Taking Issue and Allah's Answer* won the Runner-Up Prize at the Muse India Translation Awards. Dalvi is the editor of *Man without a Navel*, a collection of new and selected translations of Hemant Divate's poems from the Marathi (2018, Poetrywala). His latest book is the translation of Hemant Divate's award-winning book of poems *Paranoia*, (Poetrywala, 2023) from the Marathi. Mustansir Dalvi's translations of the poems of Faiz Ahmed Faiz, posted on his popular blog, are widely quoted, used in the media, and have been the subject of academic research.

P RIYA SARUKKAI CHABRIA is an award-winning poet, translator and writer of ten books of poetry, speculative fiction, literary non-fiction and translation and, as editor, three poetry anthologies. Her books include *Andal: The Autobiography of a Goddess* (translation), *Sing of Life* (poems), *Clone* (speculative fiction) and *Bombay/ Mumbai: Immersions* (non-fiction). Priya channels Sanskrit aesthetic theory and ancient Tamil poetics into her writing. As Founding Editor, *Poetry at Sangam* (http:// poetryatsangam. com) she is currently editing the anthology *Fafnir's Heart World Poetry in Translation*. She is the recipient of the Muse Translation Award, Kitab Experimental Fiction Award and Best Reads by Feminist Press, and has been recognised for her Outstanding Contribution to Literature by the Government of India. Her work has been widely anthologised and translated into Indian and European languages. Forthcoming are her memoir, *Archive of Absences*, and translations of the Tamil mystic Manikkavacagar. Priya is on the advisory council of WrICE Writers Immersion and Cultural Exchange, Australia.

R ANDHIR KHARE is a poet, writer, artist and educationist. His awards include the Gold Medal for Poetry from the Union of Bulgarian Writers, The Sanskriti Award For Creative Writing, The Human Rights Award, The

Dronacharaya Award for his contribution to education and The Palash Award for his lifetime contribution to Education and Culture. He has published 35 books of poetry, fiction, non-fiction, translations and educational handbooks, has had seven solo exhibitions of his art, has written/ produced/directed/performed in numerous stage shows and is a well-known folklorist and storyteller. He has produced and directed a video film titled *The World in a Story*. Doorway Film Productions has made a docu-feature on his life and work - *Makers Of God*. Randhir is Director of the Rewachand Bhojwani Academy, has been Executive Editor of *Heritage India* Magazine and is Founder-Director of The Living Heritage Movement.

RIZIO YOHANNAN RAJ is a writer, educationist, translator and governance thinker whose broad professional experience spans two decades of work in book publishing, journalism, academics and institution-building. She was Chief Executive Officer at The Marg Foundation, Mumbai and is Founder and Patron of LILA Foundation for Translocal Initiatives. She was earlier affiliated to the Malayala Manorama Group, Macmillan India, Navneet Publications, and Katha, and the Universities of Madras, Mumbai, and Kerala; and Shiv Nadar University. She has published collections of poetry, novels, critical and edited volumes, research papers and translations with reputed publishers, journals and magazines across the world.

SAMPURNA CHATTARJI is a poet, fiction-writer and translator with twenty-one books to her credit. These include the short story collection about Bombay/Mumbai *Dirty Love* (Penguin 2013); two novels *Rupture* and *Land of the Well*; and a sequence of poems *Space Gulliver: Chronicles of an Alien* (all from HarperCollins). Her translation of Joy Goswami's prose poems *After Death Comes Water* (Harper Perennial 2021) is hailed as being 'inventive and vivid as the English of Joyce'; while her translation of Sukumar Ray's poetry and prose, *Wordygurdyboom!* is a Puffin Classic. Sampurna is the editor of the anthology *Sweeping the Front Yard*, poetry and prose by women writing in English, Malayalam, Telugu and Urdu; and co-editor of *Future Library* (Red Hen Press 2022), an anthology of contemporary Indian writing released in the US. Her eleventh poetry title is *Unmappable Moves*, just out from Mumbai-based indie-press Poetrywala.

SHIKHANDIN's poems, which were originally published in the online version of *The Big Bridge Anthology of Contemporary Indian Poetry* carried her legal name, which she no longer uses as her byline. She has authored seven books, including, *The Woman on the Red Oxide Floor* (Red River Story, India), *After Grief – Poems* (Red River, India), *Impetuous Women* (Penguin-Random House India), *Immoderate Men* (Speaking Tiger), and *Vibhuti Cat* (Duckbill-Penguin-Random House India). Shikhandin is a two-time Pushcart nominee, as well as a Best of the Net nominee. She has won awards and accolades for her work in India and abroad, and her prose and poetry have been widely published worldwide in online and print journals and anthologies.

SMITA AGARWAL has been a writer in residence at the University of Stirling and the University of Kent. Her works include *Wish-granting Words, Mofussil Notebook: Poems of Small Town India, Speak, Woman!* and *Marginalized: Indian Poetry in English* (Ed.). She is also a vocalist for All-India Radio.

SUDEEP SEN is widely recognised as a major new generation voice in world literature and 'one of the finest English-language poets in the international literary scene' (*BBC Radio*), 'fascinated not just by language but the possibilities of language' (*Scotland on Sunday*). He received a Pleiades Honour (at the Struga Poetry Festival, Macedonia) for having made "a significant contribution to contemporary world poetry". His prize-winning books include: *Postmarked India: New & Selected Poems* (HarperCollins), *Rain, Aria* (A. K. Ramanujan Translation Award), *Fractals: New & Selected Poems | Translations 1980-2015* (London Magazine Editions), *EroText* (Vintage: Penguin Random House), *Kaifi Azmi: Poems | Nazms* (Bloomsbury), *Anthropocene: Climate Change, Contagion, Consolation* (Pippa Rann, 2021-22 Rabindranath Tagore Literary Prize winner), and *Red* (Nirox Foundation, 2023). He has edited influential anthologies, including: *The HarperCollins Book of English Poetry* (editor), *World English Poetry, Modern English Poetry by Younger Indians* (Sahitya Akademi), and *Converse: Contemporary English Poetry by Indians* (Pippa Rann). *Blue Nude: Ekphrasis & New Poems* (Jorge Zalamea International Poetry Prize), *The Whispering Anklets*, and *Rock* (that completes 'The Eco Trilogy') are forthcoming. Sen's works have been translated into over 25 languages. His words have appeared in the *Times Literary Supplement, Newsweek, Guardian, Observer, Independent, Telegraph*, and broadcast on BBC PBS, CNN IBN, NDTV and others. He is the editorial director of AARK ARTS, editor of *Atlas*, co-chair of Asia Pacific Writers & Translators (APWT), inaugural artist-in-residence at the Museo Camera (India), and the 2023 writer/artist-in-residence at the Nirox Foundation and Satyagraha House (South Africa). The Government of India awarded him the senior fellowship for "outstanding persons in the field of culture/literature." Sen is the first Asian honoured to deliver the Derek Walcott Lecture and read at the Nobel Laureate Festival.

TABISH KHAIR is a poet, novelist, and critic from India. Born and educated mostly in Gaya, Bihar (India), he is the author of two critically-acclaimed collections of poems, *Where Parallel Lines Meet* (Penguin, 2000) and *Man of Glass* (HarperCollins, 2010), as well as four internationally published novels, which have been shortlisted for major fiction prizes. His major books include *The Thing About Thugs*, *How to Fight Islamist Terror from the Missionary Position*, and *The Bus Stopped*. He has also won the All-India Poetry Prize and written or edited/co-edited several studies and scholarly anthologies. He teaches English literature at Aarhus University, Denmark.

TANYA MENDONSA is a poet, writer and painter. She was educated at Loreto School and College in Calcutta, India. After spending 20 years in Paris, studying French literature at the Sorbonne, painting and running a language school, she returned to India, a story told in her memoir *The Book of Joshua – The True Story of a Dog Who Loved The World*. The third edition of this memoir was published in 2020. *The Dreaming House* in 2009 was her first collection of poetry, and her second collection (both from Harper Collins), *All The Answer I Shall Ever Get*, was published in 2016. *Infinite Memories* (in collaboration with the photographer Laurence Toussaint) Editions Signum, Paris, on the city of Calcutta, was published in 2017. A third collection of poetry is forthcoming. Tanya's long poem, *The Fisher of Perch – A Fable for Our Times*, was published in book form by Paper Project (2017). Her second memoir, *A Bite In Time – Cooking with Memories*, was published by Paper Project in 2022. For two years, she wrote a column on poetry for the bi-monthly magazine *Arts Illustrated*. *The Hidden Garden*, a collection of short, haiku-like illustrated poems, will be published online in 2024.

TISHANI DOSHI is an award-winning poet, novelist and dancer whose work centres the body as a vehicle to explore gender, sexuality and power. Her publications include *Girls Are Coming Out of the Woods*, *Small Days and Nights*, and *A God at the Door*. She is a fellow of the Royal Society of Literature and a Visiting Associate Professor at New York University, Abu Dhabi.

VIHANG A. NAIK (1969-2021) published four collections of poetry. They included *Poetry Manifesto: New & Selected Poems*, *Making A Poem*, *City Times and Other Poems* and *Jeevangeet* (Gujarati). He also translated poetry from Gujarati into English, including his own Gujarati language poems. He attended the Maharaja Sayajirao University of Baroda with English Literature, Indian Literature in English Translation and Philosophy. Vihang received several awards for his poetry including the Michael Madhusudan Dutt Prize, Beverly Hills Book Award 2016, Book Excellence Award 2017 and Konark Literary Fest Award 2019. In 2016, his poetry collection *City Times and Other Poems* entered the *Limca Book of Records* for the poem *Self Portrait*, which was composed of only five blank pages.

2015

ABHAY K. is the author of a memoir and a dozen poetry books including *Celestial* (Mapin 2023), *Stray Poems* (Poetrywala, 2022), *Monsoon* (Sahitya Akademi,

India, 2022), *La Magie de Madagascar/The Magic of Madagascar* (L'Harmattan, Paris, 2021), *The Alphabets of Latin America* (Bloomsbury India, 2020), *The Prophecy of Brasilia* (Coletivo Editorial, Brazil, 2018) *The Eight-Eyed Lord of Kathmandu* (Bloomsbury India, 2018 |The Onslaught Press, UK), *The Seduction Of Delhi* (Bloomsbury India, 2014). He has edited *CAPITALS* (Bloomsbury India 2017); *The Bloomsbury Anthology of Great Indian Poems, The Bloomsbury Book of Great Indian Love Poems* (2020) and *The Book of Bihari Literature* (HarperCollins India 2022). His *100 Great Indian Poems* have been translated and published into Portuguese (*100 Grandes Poemas da India*), Spanish (*Cien Grandes Poemas de la India*), Italian (*100 Grandi Poesie Indiane*), Malagasy, French, Arabic and Greek. He has also translated and edited *New Brazilian Poems*. His translations include Kalidasa's *Meghaduta* (Bloomsbury India) and *Ritusamhara* (Bloomsbury India). His translation of the first Magahi novel *Fool Bahadur* into English has been published by Penguin India as a Modern Classic. His forthcoming book is titled *Nalanda*, which will be published by Penguin Random House in 2025.

ANITA NAIR is the internationally acclaimed author of the novels *The Better Man, Ladies Coupe, Mistress, Lessons in Forgetting* **and** *Cut Like Wound*. She has also published a collection of poems titled *Malabar Mind* and a collection of essays titled *Goodnight & God Bless*, and has written two plays and the screenplay for the movie adaptation of her novel *Lessons in Forgetting* which won the National Film Award for 2012. She was awarded the Central Sahitya Akademi award for her contribution to Children's Literature in 2013. Her books have been translated into thirty-two languages around the world and have been adapted for audio, the stage and the screen. Founder of the creative writing mentorship programme Anita's Attic which has mentored over 125 writers, Anita Nair is also a High-Profile Supporter of the UNHCR. Anita Nair's new novel is *Hot Stage*, third in the Borei Gowda noir series.

ANJALI PUROHIT is a painter, writer, poet, translator and curator. She is the author of two books, *Ragi Ragini: Chronicles from Aji's Kitchen* (Yoda Press, 2012) and *Go Talk to the River: The Ovis of Bahinabai Choudhari* (Yoda Press, 2019). She is the founder and curator of *The Cappuccino Adda* (formerly the *Cappuccino Readings*), an initiative working to foster a literary café culture in Mumbai and to contribute towards building a vibrant writers' community.

ANNA SUJATHA MATHAI (1934 - 2023) studied English Literature at the University of Delhi, and later at Bangalore. She completed a Post-Graduate degree in Social Studies from the University of Edinburgh, and worked in the U.K. in this field. Her passion was the Theatre, but cut off by circumstances, and in an isolated situation, she started writing poetry - and throwing it away! However, an ad in a paper by an American professor asking for "poems from avant-garde writers" led to her sending him a few. His reply that he was "moved" encouraged her to continue writing. She published five collections of poetry in English, and read at venues across the world. Many of her poems have been translated into Indian and European languages. The poems represented here were first published in *The Attic of the Night* (Rupa. 1991), and *On My Side of the Street*, in the Sahitya Akademi's 50th Anniversary Special Issue. In 2018, she received the WE Kamala Das award. She passed away on March 16, 2023.

BARNALI RAY SHUKLA is a filmmaker, writer and a poet. Her writing has featured in the *Indian Quarterly, Gallerie, Sunflower Collective, Out of Print, Kitaab.org, On Eating, Madras Courier, Bengaluru Review, Indian Ruminations, Vayavya, The Punch Magazine, The Brown Critique, Kaurab, Usawa Literary Review, Portside Review, Anthology of Contemporary Indian Poetry II*, indianculturalforum.in, *Modern English Poetry By Younger Indians* (Sahitya Akademi), *The World That Belongs To Us* (Harper Collins India), *Have A Safe Journey* (Amaryllis), *Side Effects Of Living* (Speaking Tiger), *Hibiscus* (Hawakal), *Open Your Eyes* (Hawakal), *The Kali Project* (Indie Blu-e Publishing), *Converse: Contemporary English Poetry By Indians* (PippaRann Books & Media), *Rivers Going Home* (Indian Novels Collective & Red River Press), *The YearBook of Indian Poetry in English* 2020 & 2022 (Hawakal), *Borderless* (Singapore), *Voice & Verse* (Hong Kong), *UCityReview* (USA), *A Portrait in Blues* (UK), and *Centre for Stories* (Australia). She has two feature films as a writer-director, three documentaries, and two short films, as well as a book of poems, *Apostrophe* (RLFPA). Her new Hindi feature film, *Joon*, premiered in Bolivia, has bagged 17 awards across film festivals in Bolivia, Brazil, Norway, Sweden, France, Japan, USA, Indonesia, Turkey, Bulgaria, UK and India. Now slated for an OTT release later this year.

DEEPANKAR KHIWANI (1971 – 2020) was born in 1971 in New Delhi. He read Economics at Bombay University, and took postgraduate degrees in accounting and in business management. He lived in Paris, where he worked for a consulting and technology services company. Deepankar's first book of poems, *Entr'acte*, was published in 2006 by the Harbour Line collective. His book, *de Kooning's Smile: Collected Poems* (Copper Coin), appeared posthumously in 2023. In 2024, the Drunken Boat Global Classics series featured his work in *Three Indian Poets: Arundhathi Subramaniam, Deepankar Khiwani and Anand Thakore*. The Vampire of the Underground featured here is from *Entr›acte*. Deepankar passed away in March 2020. With the help of generous donors, The Quarantine Train has instituted the Deepankar Khiwani Memorial Prize to honour his memory.

DION D'SOUZA is a poet and short fiction writer. He is the author of *Three Doors* (Poetrywala, 2016), a collection of poems, and the poetry chapbook *Mirrors Lie*, and *Sometimes Mothers* (Yavanika Press, 2021). He lives in Bombay, India.

DOMINIC ALAPAT is the author of *Howling Through the Universe*, a book of poems published on amazon.com in 2023. His earlier books of poetry include *Reeling* (2012), *Circling the Sky* (2013), *The Branches* (2015), *New and Selected Poems* (2016) and *Lame Blind Dog* (2023), all published online. His poems have appeared in *Nthposition, decomP, Kavya Bharati, Nether* and *Tipton Poetry Journal*, among other poetry zines. The poems here originally appeared in *Reeling* (2012).

GJV PRASAD, formerly Professor of English at Jawaharlal Nehru University, is a writer, critic, and translator. He has translated two books from Tamil to English – Ambai's *A Red-necked Green Bird* (2021), and Imayam's *A Woman Burnt* (2023), which received the KLF Award for Translation.

GOPIKRISHNAN KOTTOOR has won national awards for his poetry such as the All India Poetry Society - British Council Poetry Awards in all categories (various years), Wingword International prize and honourable mentions (various years), Chandigarh Lit fest awards (various years) and more. He has published his poetry in journals and anthologies of repute both in India and abroad. His poetry has been translated into German, Hindi, Sinhalese, Tamil, Odisha, Mandarin and Telugu, among others. His oeuvre includes novels, *(A Bridge Over Karma, Presumed Guilty, The Anklet) plays, (The Mask of Death - The Final Days of John Keats, Fire in the Soul - The Life and Times of Subramania Bharati, The Nectar of the Gods - The Life and Times of the Layman Saint and Martyr St. Devasahayam)* and translations *(Jnanappana of Poonthanam, Ramanan, the Pastoral by Changampuzha)*. He edited *A New Book of Indian Poems in English*, and recently, *Living Poetry, Seven Kerala Poets Writing in English*. Kottoor has published twenty poetry collections including the recent *Krishna, and Other Poems*. His forthcoming poetry collections are *This Small Town*, and *Poems from America and Other Poems*. He founded Poetry Chain, and now edits its online poetry journal *Chipmunk*. He retired as a senior banker with Reserve Bank of India and lives in Trivandrum, Kerala.

JENNIFER ROBERTSON is a poet, critic, and consultant based in Mumbai. Her poems have been published in the US, UK, and India: *Poetry magazine* (USA), *Emma Press* (UK), *The Missing Slate* (USA), *Domus* (India), *Almost Island* (India) and others. Many of her poems have been widely anthologised: *40 Under 40: An Anthology Of Post-Globalization Poetry; Modern English Poetry by Younger Indians* published by Sahitya Akademi and *The Penguin Book of Indian*

Poets. Her critical essays and book reviews have appeared in *The American Book Review, Scroll, The Telegraph* and elsewhere. Jennifer has convened the literary chapter for the PEN All-India Centre at Prithvi Theatre. Her debut poetry collection *Folie a deux* has been published in the USA (Everybody Press, 2023) and is forthcoming in India (Paperwall Publishing, 2024).

LINDA ASHOK is an Indian English poet. Author of *Whorelight, Waiting for the Helicopter*, and *Sharpless 29*. She introduced the Best Indian Poetry 2018 and sponsored the RL Poetry Award from 2013 to 2019. Currently, Linda is based in Kolkata, studying to pivot as a clinical psychologist.

MALSAWMI JACOB writes poems in two languages and has translated a few short pieces between Mizo language and English. She also writes fiction and articles, has published 10 books in different genres and contributed to several publications. Her novel *Zorami A Redemption Song* is prescribed reading for postgraduates in some universities and used by scholars as part of their research material. Earlier, she had taught English to undergraduates in Bengaluru and Aizawl, worked as Senior Coordinator with Sound and Picture Archives for Research on Women (SPARROW) Mumbai, and freelanced with newspapers such as *The Statesman, The Assam Tribune, The Telegraph (Northeast)* and *Northeast Frontier* magazine. She now lives alternately in Bengaluru and Kumbanad, a Kerala village.

MANI RAO is the author of eleven poetry books including *Sing to Me* (Recent Work Press Australia), and *New & Selected Poems* (Poetrywala); three books in translation including *Saundarya Lahari - Wave of Beauty* (HarperCollins 2023) and *Bhagavad Gita - God's Song* (HarperCollins 2022); and an academic book *Living Mantra* (Palgrave Macmillan 2019). Her poems and essays are in numerous journals and anthologies including W.W.Norton's *Language for a New Century* and the *Bloodaxe Book of Contemporary Indian Poets*. Mani has an MFA in Creative Writing, and a PhD in religious studies.

MANISHA LAKHE has been writing ever since she can remember. she has worked across all media starting with advertising copywriting. she stumbled into journalism, jumped into the web, pushing magazines into the digital age, has built web communities for clients. It was her passion that led her to create Caferati, an online forum for writers, which has grown from 16 writers sharing their work on a stormy afternoon to more than 5,000 people world-wide, spread across 22 cities sharing their works online. She's currently writing sangria-fuelled screenplays and her second novel.

NABINA DAS' latest poetry collection *Anima and the Narrative Limits* is from Yoda Press. Her other poetry collections are *Sanskarnama* (Red River, 2017), *Into the Migrant City* (Writers Workshop, 2013), *and Blue Vessel* (Les Editions du Zaporogue, 2012). Her debut book is a novel titled *Footprints in the Bajra (Cedar Books, 2010)*, and her short fiction volume is titled *The House of Twining Roses: Stories of the Mapped and the Unmapped* (LiFi Publications, 2014). Her first book of translations, titled *Arise out of the Lock: 50 Bangladeshi Women Poets in English* (curated by Alam Khorshed, Chittagong), appeared in early 2022 from Balestier Press, UK. A Rutgers-Camden MFA alumna, Nabina is the editor of *WITNESS, The Red River Book of Poetry of Dissent* (Red River, 2021), and co-editor of *40 under 40, an Anthology of Post-globalisation Poetry* (Poetrywala, 2016). Nabina is a 2017 Sahapedia-UNESCO fellow, a 2012 Charles Wallace Creative Writing alumna (Stirling University, Scotland), and a 2016 Commonwealth Writers features correspondent. Born and brought up in Guwahati, Assam, she is a 2012 Sangam House, a 2011 NYS Summer Writers Institute, and a 2007 Wesleyan Writers Conference creative writing alumna.

ROCHELLE POTKAR is an author, poet, and screenwriter. She is the author of *Four Degrees of Separation* (poetry) *Paper Asylum* (haibun) – shortlisted for the Rabindranath Tagore Literary Prize 2020, *Bombay Hangovers* (story fiction), and *Coins in Rivers* (poetry, Hachette India). Prize-winning and widely anthologized, she is an alumna of Iowa's International Writing Program and a Charles Wallace Writer's fellow, University of Stirling. She was a creative-writing teacher four times in a row, at Iowa's prestigious International Writing Programs: Summer Institute 2019 and Between the Lines 2022, 2023, and 2024, and conducts regular online poetry workshops at the Himalayan Writing Retreat. She is also an emerging screenwriter, with a few of her screenplays nominated for prizes.

SARABJEET GARCHA is a poet, editor, translator and publisher. His five books of poems include *All We Have* and *A Clock in the Far Past*, in addition to a volume each of poems translated from Marathi and prose translated from Hindi. *The Necropolis Trilogy*, a translation of three long essays by the iconic Marathi playwright Mahesh Elkunchwar, is his latest book. He has translated several

American poets into Hindi, including W. S. Merwin and John Haines, and several Indian poets into English, among them Mangalesh Dabral and Leeladhar Jagoori. His poems, translations and essays have been published in the *Notre Dame Review, Versopolis, Lyrikline, Modern Poetry in Translation, Asymptote, Two Lines Journal, the Indian Quarterly, Scroll, the Wire,* among other publications and several anthologies. He has received the Fellowship for Outstanding Artists from the Government of India, the International Publishing Fellowship from the British Council, and the inaugural Godyo Podyo Probondho Award. His poems have been translated into German, Spanish, Russian, Malayalam, Kannada, Marathi, Punjabi and Hindi. He is the founder and editorial director of Copper Coin, a multilingual publishing company based in Delhi NCR.

SHIKHA MALAVIYA is a poet, writer and mentor. Her book of historical persona poetry, *Anandibai Joshee: A Life in Poems* (HarperCollins India, 2023) is a unique retelling of the life of India's first female medical doctor and the first Indian woman to study medicine in the United States. Shikha's previous book of poems, *Geography of Tongues,* was published to acclaim in 2014. Her poetry has been nominated for the Pushcart Prize and featured in *Catamaran, PLUME, Prairie Schooner* & other fine publications. Shikha has been a featured TEDx speaker and was selected as Poet Laureate of San Ramon, California, 2016. Shikha is co-founder of The (Great) Indian Poetry Collective, a mentorship-model literary press and is currently a Mosaic America Fellow. She lives in the San Francisco Bay area with her family.

SRIDALA SWAMI is the author of three collections of poetry, including the recent *Run for the Shadows* (Context/ Westland: 2021, reprinted 2022). She has served on the Jury of the Montreal International Poetry Prize (2019) and on the Rayaprol Poetry Prize (2023). She lives in Hyderabad.

UMA NARAYAN was Professor of Philosophy and Andrew W. Mellon Chair of the Humanities at Vassar College, New York until she retired in 2022. She is the author of *Dislocating Cultures: Identities, Traditions and Third World Feminism*, which won the Victoria Schuk award for the best book on women and politics in 1997. She has edited three anthologies - *Reconstructing Political Theory: Feminist Perspectives, Having and Raising Children* and *Deconstructing the Center: Feminist, Multicultural and Postcolonial Challenges to Philosophy*. She has written poetry for years and is now starting to make it a part of her public life.

USHA AKELLA has authored five books of poetry, three chapbooks, and scripted/produced two musical dramas. She earned an MSt in Creative Writing from the University of Cambridge, UK (2018). She is the host of a curated interviews website *www.the-pov.com*. She is the founder and director of Matwaala (*www.matwaala.com*) a festival and collective initiated to increase the visibility of South Asian poets in the USA.

Black Eagle Books

www.blackeaglebooks.org
info@blackeaglebooks.org

Black Eagle Books, an independent publisher, was founded as a nonprofit organization in April, 2019. It is our mission to connect and engage the Indian diaspora and the world at large with the best of works of world literature published on a collaborative platform, with special emphasis on foregrounding Contemporary Classics and New Writing.

MENKA SHIVDASANI

Menka Shivdasani, a Mumbai-based poet, editor and translator, is the author of five poetry collections. Her first book of poems in 1990, *Nirvana at Ten Rupees* was published by Adil Jussawalla and described by Bruce King as "one of the best first books of poetry to appear during the 1990s." (*Modern Indian Poetry in English, Revised Edition*, OUP, 2001). She subsequently published *Stet* (2001), *Safe House* (2015) and *Frazil* (1990-2017). Her most recent work, *The Seven Queens*, a retelling of Sindhi folktales in English verse, was published in 2024.

She has co-translated *Freedom and Fissures*, an anthology of Sindhi Partition poetry (Sahitya Akademi, 1998), and edited *If the Roof Leaks, Let it Leak*, an anthology of women's writing for Sound and Picture Archives for Research on Women (2014).

A widely published poet, Menka's work has been included in the Second Year Bachelor of Arts textbook of the University of Mumbai. She has also worked extensively to promote Sindhi literature and has collaborated with the senior Sindhi poet Mohan Gehani on three of his poetry collections in English translation. A poem by her, based on a Sindhi folktale, has been made into a short film by noted filmmaker Susheel Gajwani.

Menka's awards include the Ethos Literary Award (2019) and the inaugural WE Eunice de Souza Award (2020). She was a finalist for the Rabindranath Tagore Literary Prize in 2019. As a literary curator, Menka co-founded Poetry Circle in Bombay in 1986, co-founded and curated the Culture Beat activities of the Mumbai Press Club for more than a decade, and has organized poetry festivals for 100 Thousand Poets for Change since 2011.

Menka is Co-Chair, Asia Pacific Writers and Translators (APWT). Her work as a journalist includes 18 books, co-authored/edited with Raju Kane, three of which were released by the then Indian Prime Minister Atal Bihari Vajpayee.

MICHAEL ROTHENBERG

Michael Rothenberg (1951-2022) was a poet, artist, songwriter, editor and environmentalist. In 1989, he began Big Bridge Press, which published works by Jim Harrison, Allen Ginsberg and Philip Whalen, among others. Big Bridge Magazine, the webzine started in 1997, was among the earliest online literary journals. Michael also helped create Poets in Need, a group providing emergency funds to poets in crisis. In 2011, he co-founded 100 Thousand Poets for Change with Terri Carrion, a global movement focused on issues of peace, justice and sustainability. They also went on to establish the 'Read A Poem To A Child' initiative. Rothenberg published over 20 books of poetry, most recently *In Memory of A Banyan Tree, Poems of the Outside World, 1985-2020* (Lost Horse Press) *I Murdered Elvis*, (Alien Buddha Press) *The Pillars* (Quaranzine Press) and *Drawing the Shade* (Dos Madres Press). His editorial work includes several volumes in the Penguin Poets series: *Overtime* by Philip Whalen and *As Ever* by Joanne Kyger. He was also editor of *The Collected Poems of Philip Whalen* published by Wesleyan University Press. Rothenberg recorded two spoken word CDs in collaboration with prominent musicians. He was Florida State University Libraries Poet in Residence; the FSU Special Collections and Archives now house his personal papers. Rothenberg died of lung cancer on November 21, 2022.

www.ingramcontent.com/pod-product-compliance
Lightning Source LLC
Chambersburg PA
CBHW060553080526
44585CB00013B/545